WE SHALL GROW

WE SHALL GROW

A collection on the themes of life, love and creativity

Edited by Keenan Brookland
Art by Slate Bender

Trafford Publishing   *   Bloomington, Indiana

Trafford rev. 09/22/2011

 www.trafford.com

North America & international
toll-free: 1 888 232 4444 (USA & Canada)
phone: 250 383 6864 ♦ fax: 812 355 4082

A Note

Thanks to an increasingly global economy where we can speak daily with people around the planet, this collection includes helpings of poetry from the east as well as stories and poetry from the west.

The whimsical art of Slate Bender is woven throughout, with simplicity and humor that makes us smile.

The common themes of these artists are love, creative communication and the dream of a better world.

Table of Contents

We Shall Grow

By Amit Kapoor

To the crusader of peace outside Capital Hall, Lucknow

You are not alone, Sir,
We the youth are with you,
If you want happiness, spread it—
Got the clue?

Some of us have lost our souls,
In the race for money, misplaced our goals,
But, some live, still, just for others,
Caring for their countrymen, their brothers.

Though the rate is slow,
But, be assured—we shall grow—
Grow into one united nation,
Without any creeds or vulgar fashions.

A day will come when humanity will rise,
Believe me, Sir, and don't get surprised,
That day, Love shall reign supreme on our skies,
Where the peaceful, white dove flies.

A Vision or a Dream?

By Keenan Brookland, 2006

In a tranquil slumbering moment
I was once in another place.
I walked through an amber lit forest
hand in hand with a dear one.

We were at peace.
There was companionship, hope, love
and no encroachment of evil or jealousy.

The atmosphere itself was free of
the clouds of misery and hopelessness
we so often feel here on earth.
We didn't fear criminality would approach.
We didn't suffer for the hungry and
addicted because there were none.

The collective minds and spirits of the planet
on which we walked were as happy as we.

Although I awoke, I cannot believe
it was not real.
It was more real than anything else in my life.

You

By Amit Kapoor

You,
Stand alone
In the queue,
With an innocence of
The first drops
Of dew.

You,
Beautiful enchantress,
Divine,
With eyes
As intoxicating as
Wine.

You, sweet beloved,
Cute,
With a voice
As soothing as the
Flute.

You,
Mature, poised,
Funny,
With a constitution,
Calm, composed, and
Sunny.

You, my trust, fidelity,
Belief,
With arms
To hold me, giving
Relief.

You,
My mirth, ecstasy,
Life,
With all my love
I propose—be my
Wife.

Unexpected Gifts

By Kendall Roman, 1995

Even though it was Christmas Eve, maybe *especially* because it was Christmas Eve and he was alone, the warmth of the fire was of no comfort to him and the years of collected ornaments lit up intermittently by Christmas tree lights had no charm for him. This had once been Gareth's favorite day of the year. Ten years ago exactly he had married Beth, right in front of this very hearth. She was as enthusiastic as he was about a Christmas wedding. The Maid of Honor wore red velvet and every corner of the house seemed filled with echoes of the busy feet of nieces and nephews. That was as it should be, Gareth thought.

Gareth's family had been especially happy at his marriage. He was younger than his brothers and sisters by five years, and his mother had wondered if he would ever start a family of his own or would stay devoted to his books and dreams of writing for the rest of his life. He never seemed interested in girls, but suddenly one day he announced his engagement to Beth, right after he graduated from the University. His family was taken by surprise, but very happy.

Ten years ago he had imagined quite a different future for himself. He expected that his own children's laughter would soon replace that of his nieces and nephews, as both he and Beth looked forward to having children. Not a single child had been born to them after three years of marriage, but when Gareth tried to encourage Beth to see a doctor about it she assured him nothing was wrong and if they were patient the right time would come. She seemed so confident that he decided not to doubt her.

After five years of marriage she had a career she liked very much: consulting for large businesses and helping them straighten out their organizational difficulties. Whenever he brought up the subject of children she said, "It's just as well we haven't had a child yet because I have to spend so much time with my clients while I'm earning my reputation." She began going out of town, sometimes for several weeks, to handle larger and larger businesses. It did not seem to diminish her feelings for him in any way, and she seemed so happy with her work that he couldn't question the rightness of it. He loved to hear her talk about how she had solved various problems and what she had learned about "the peculiarities of human nature," as she put it. Mainly he just liked to see her happy.

His own career was a different matter altogether. He had imagined that he would have *some* degree of success as a writer, but after five years of submissions of stories and even two novels he had not had a single thing published. He felt his first duty was to support himself and his wife so he had always held a full time job and kept his writing in his spare time. For six years now he had worked at a large hardware store nearby, and had acquired the reputation in his neighborhood as the man to go to for advice and help in home maintenance problems. While this did not give him any added income, it made him feel useful and kept his life busy when his wife was out of town. It also created tremendous good will for him and he had many visitors come with homemade gifts of thanks.

Somehow the writing had faded out of his life. It had been three years since he had sent something to a publisher, and that was a science fiction story to the *Sci-Fiction Addiction* magazine. He never even got a rejection slip from them. After that he always meant to get back to it some day, but never seemed to have the time. He had developed skills in repairing plumbing, putting up new walls, and fixing electrical wiring, and someone was forever needing his help on some project or another.

As it was Christmas Eve and nine o'clock already, Gareth put on some Christmas music and made some eggnog to go with the cookies the neighbor children had brought him. Beth's plane had been snowed in and this unexpectedly left him alone for their anniversary while she traveled by car to try to make it home before Christmas Day was over. He let his mind drift over Christmases past, but this only tended to make him a bit melancholy.

I Heard the Bells on Christmas Day came over the radio. When he heard the words "Peace on Earth, Good will toward men," he recalled the first time he had come to any understanding of that phrase. It was on a Christmas Day when he was perhaps seven years old at most. He and his brother were fighting over some new toy one of them had received for Christmas. Normally his mother would have cut it short with a reprimand, but on this day she was in an exceptionally good mood. With no irritation or scolding she simply asked them to come over and sit by her. She asked them if they knew why they were celebrating Christmas. The older brother mumbled something he had learned at school, but basically neither one of them had much to say. They were still half expecting the usual reprimand and now felt even more guilty for the intellectual sin of not knowing the answer to what they sensed was an important question.

Gareth's mother was not a religious woman, but she was an imaginative one. She proceeded to tell them all the Christmas stories they had missed by not attending church. Santa Claus and Rudolph were old acquaintances due to television and school experiences, but the Virgin Mary, Three Kings and Christ in the Manger were personages they had maybe heard of but never comprehended. She was always careful to preface each explanation with lines such as, "Some people believe this is true and others believe it is only a story..." so that they did not later become confused. She told the stories quite beautifully and dramatically, making it clear to them the significance of a Messiah to a people who had been oppressed for so many hundreds of years. As she had studied history well, she could fill in the details in such a way that the stories seemed realistic to two young boys who had not long ago been thoroughly engaged in human avarice and greed.

As well as being entertaining, their mother's stories also cleared up for them numerous things they had not understood about certain Christmas carols. She had just finished explaining "The Little Drummer Boy" to them when she quietly suggested that they each prepare a gift in honor of the man who brought to so many people the message, "Love your neighbor as yourself" and helped make life happier.

Gareth chose to write a story. In fact it was the first story he wrote and was in one sense the beginning of his determination to be a writer some day. He wrote a story of Knights and Castles and Dragons, remembering all the tales his mother had told him of the Knight for which he was named. He had always had a particular affinity for these legends and asked to hear them often; eventually he read them again and again for himself.

It was only when he heard the phone ring and saw the clock that Gareth realized he must have dozed off. It was two o'clock in the morning.

Annoyance gave way to mild panic when he recalled that his wife was driving through the worst of weather to reach him by Christmas. What if she were trying to drive all night and something had happened?

He jumped over to the phone and grabbed it, trying to say hello into it as calmly as possible. All he heard on the other end was raspy breathing and faint shuffling sounds; then it sounded as if the phone fell to the floor.

Adrenaline shot through him as he imagined what might be wrong with his wife. He shouted into the receiver for several seconds but then made up his mind to go immediately to Beth's office phone and have the call traced. He could barely speak clearly enough to be understood once he reached the operator, but somehow managed to get her cooperation. He explained the situation and asked her to get the address of the phone originating the call on his other line so he could get an ambulance sent.

Those few moments while he waited passed as slowly as ten lifetimes. He thought of the ten years he'd spent with Beth, feeling stricken at the thought that they might come to an end so prematurely before they had even had any children together, before they'd celebrated all the anniversaries they had imagined together on distant Christmas Eves, before they had enjoyed grandchildren together.

He tried to push such thoughts away and decide that of course she would be all right, of course she would because after all she had managed to call him. This was their anniversary, this was Christmas, and nothing so tragic could possibly happen.

"Have you got a pencil?" the Operator asked suddenly. Gareth grabbed a pen from his desk and got a message pad.

"Yes," he said.

"Here's the number," she said, as if to a child. "208-373-7072. The address is 1520 West Holt Street."

He obediently wrote it down. "I'm sending an ambulance now," she said finally.

"Thank you," he mumbled, and hung up.

Only after he had run to the closet for his coat did he look closely at the address. It was a local phone number and the address was in an area several miles away. It did not make sense. Why would his wife be in that area if she was driving from Tremonton?

He stopped in his tracks as more petrifying possibilities occurred to him. He forced himself to continue. Better to find out sooner than later, whatever it was. He started his car, numb to the cold and feeling almost nauseous. Within a few minutes he was crunching his way through frozen snow, heading toward 1520 West Holt Street. An occasional house was lit, its inhabitants partying into the early hours of the morning, but the streets were quiet otherwise. He wondered if this were a nightmare and tried to will himself to wake up. He did not wake up. He continued driving through the unreal atmosphere.

When he arrived, the ambulance attendants were carrying someone on a stretcher from the house to the vehicle. He parked and walked to the ambulance. What he saw did not make sense. The woman they carried was wearing an oxygen mask but her white hair and frailness identified her positively as "not Beth." His relief was instantaneous, but followed by confusion. He verified that the address was indeed 1520 West Holt Street. Why did this woman--*or someone*--call him?

The ambulance attendants had her safely inside and the driver was heading toward his seat when he noticed Gareth.

"Do you need any help?" Gareth asked, so as not to look like a mere gawker.

The driver assessed him quickly and then tossed him a small flower-covered address book. "If you've got a cell phone you could call her family. We're taking her to Treasure Valley Hospital." Gareth copied down the number and gave the book back to the attendant as he jumped in and they drove off.

Gareth did not have a cell phone. He went to the nearest phone booth he could find and dialed the number listed under the line "In Case of Emergency". As he dialed he realized what had happened. The phone number was identical to his with the exception of one digit. The woman must have made a mistake in her dialing and reached him instead of the person she intended.

"Hello," said a very hoarse feminine voice; hoarse with the sound of just having woken up.

Gareth paused a second as he now remembered that he didn't know the name of the woman in the ambulance. "Hello," he said. "I'm very sorry but an elderly woman has just been taken to the hospital due to a stroke and yours is the number listed in her book to notify in case of emergency."

"Oh my God, oh my God!" she cried. "Is she all right? Where is she?"

"I only saw her briefly," Gareth replied, "but they were administering oxygen and she seemed to be conscious. They are on the way to Treasure Valley Hospital."

"Thank you!" She hung up violently.

Gareth hung up, feeling some of the woman's panic by contagion. He decided to drive to the hospital. He had to return the address book anyway, and he might as well try to be of some comfort or use to someone as long as he was awake.

When he arrived in the Emergency entrance to the hospital he inquired after the elderly woman and found that she was being admitted and apparently in serious but not critical condition. The Receptionist assumed he was family and started asking him questions needed for the Admissions paperwork.

"I was only a bystander when the ambulance came," he explained. "I don't know her, but I called a relative—"

Before he could finish his sentence they both turned to note the approach of a dark-haired woman who rushed in the door and asked, as soon as she had the attention of the Receptionist, "Where is Cecilia Whitney?" Her hair was uncombed, her facial expression streamlined by urgency and absent of make-up. She wore a long casual tunic with boots under a heavy coat.

The Receptionist explained that she was with her Doctor right now, doing as well as could be expected and that she needed to complete the Admissions paperwork.

"Can I see her first?" she pleaded.

"Not quite yet," the Receptionist answered gently. "But I'll let the nurse know you're here and she will call you in as soon as possible." She made the appropriate call while the woman breathed deeply, paced, stretched and used other such methods to try to relieve herself of stress.

Gareth stood awkwardly in the background, waiting for an appropriate moment to present itself. As the Receptionist prepared to launch into the paperwork, he interrupted briefly to ask the woman if he could get her something hot to drink.

She became aware of him for the first time. "Why thank you, that would be wonderful," she said gratefully. "Tea with cream and sugar, please," and she offered him a crumpled dollar bill from her pocket.

He refused the money, saying, "Please let me," as he walked off. The Receptionist handed her a form.

When Gareth returned she was still writing. He brought the tea to her and she smiled at him and said simply "Thank you." He drank a cup of coffee, waiting for her to finish. She joined him when she finished the last form.

"Is your person doing all right?" she asked delicately.

"Oh, I don't have a person here," he explained. "I mean, my person is the same as yours. I'm the man who called you about her."

"Oh? How did you—what is your—"

He began to explain, relieving her of the necessity of asking the right question. "Mrs. Whitney called my number instead of yours. She was not able to speak, so I had the call traced and the Operator sent an ambulance to her address."

"Oh," said the woman, now understanding. "I thank you so *very* much. Not everyone would have gone to that much trouble. What is your name?"

"Gareth Brooks. And yours?"

"Emma Runick. I'm very glad to meet you." She gave him her hand and he clasped it. "Why did you come to the hospital?"

"To make myself useful. My wife is on her way home from a business trip and won't arrive until tomorrow. When I got the mysterious call it worked too much on my imagination, and I prefer this to tossing and turning at home, worried about my wife's safety."

Emma nodded in agreement. "I know how it is to worry. My grandmother is my major worry these days. It is important for me to keep track of her because she is quite old and lives alone. I tried to get her to live with me but she won't have anything to do with that idea. I did at least convince her to register with the Emergency Network so that authorized attendants can enter her home in just such emergencies as these, while her house remains protected from unauthorized intruders. I shudder when I read of crimes against helpless elderly people."

Emma sipped her tea and then asked, "What was your name again?"

"Gareth Brooks."

"That sounds so familiar. Where might I know you from?"

"I work in the hardware store on Empire street. Most people know me as the person to ask about home repairs, but other than that I'm afraid I'm not very noteworthy."

"Don't say that!" she said, and smiled warmly. He felt a rush of emotion and a sense of wonder at the tie that binds all humans together in the quest for mutual survival. "Gareth Brooks...," she mused aloud, "I know I've heard that name. I just can't think of where right now. Maybe I'll remember by tomorrow. I like to remember things like this because nothing ever happens around my grandmother by coincidence. She is a real character in that respect. When she decides that things are going to happen, they *happen*. She would take it as an insult if you didn't believe that it was her decision that made it happen! Sometimes events lead up to her decisions in very unexpected ways, but she takes it all in stride and knows it will all come out in the end. And it does, remarkably enough."

"She sounds like some kind of Divinity!" Gareth remarked.

"I should tell you," answered Emma, "that she doesn't decide about *all* kinds of things. We used to try to get her to 'decide' we were going to win the prize, or be asked to the prom, or whatever our childish whims were—my sisters and I, that is—but Grandma would only say, 'That's not my department.' I would be hard-pressed to decide which she said more often: '*Nothing* is a coincidence,' or 'That's not my department.'"

Gareth smiled. "What *is* her department?" he asked.

"Sometimes it was her family and their livelihood, sometimes it was local politics. She was very often outspoken in community issues, but not really in larger scale issues. And she *never* interfered with her husband and his decisions, even when she disagreed with them. Recently, now that I think about it, the only thing she's gotten adamant about is her own death."

She paused a few moments in thought and with genuine curiosity Gareth said, "What did she say about that?"

"Well, she mainly didn't want anyone making a fuss about it or trying to keep her alive as a vegetable, or spending a lot of money and grief on her after she was gone. 'I'll be insulted if you don't just get on with life,' she would say. And she meant it. She's not a sympathy-loving sort, and I can imagine that the thought of people mourning over her would seem a shameful waste to her; almost a humiliation that people would respond to her memory that way instead of getting busy."

"That's a practical viewpoint," said Gareth.

"Yes, she *is* practical. She just had one request of Fate, and that was that she die quickly and with someone present. She wants it to be me. She's stationed herself in my vicinity now that she feels her life is coming to a close. It was hard for me to get used to at first, but I've come to think of it as a duty. I must keep my promise to be with her when she dies. In the mean time, I still greatly enjoy her company and don't want that moment to come at all soon."

Gareth replied quietly, "I understand," seeing that Beth was struggling with an outbreak of tears that wanted release. She at last succumbed and sobbed silently for a brief time. Gareth squeezed her shoulders briefly to acknowledge her emotion. She looked at him and made an attempt to smile.

"Mrs. Runick," said a Doctor to the chart in his hand. Emma walked over to him immediately and he explained the results of his examination to her. It was quite possible that Cecilia would recover completely in time, but it was too early to tell for sure. She was sleeping comfortably now and Emma could visit her tomorrow.

"Can I just see her quickly right now?" she asked.

"Well, I suppose we could arrange that, but please don't disturb her sleep," he said.

"Of course not," she answered. The Doctor went off to make arrangements and Emma turned to Gareth. "Thank you for coming here. If there's anything I can do for you, please let me know."

"All right. But I'm very glad to have helped. Do you need any help getting home in this weather?"

"Oh no, I'm fine. Thank you again."

They parted and Gareth slept soundly once he returned home. By noon he was awake, dressed and breakfasted. Several people dropped by to bring him gifts or holiday greetings, but still the time passed far too slowly as he waited for Beth to arrive. She finally called at around three to say she would arrive in a couple of hours. They made plans for the rest of the day and she said mysteriously, "You will be glad, wait and see!"

"What are you trying to hide from me?" he said to tease her.

"Your Christmas present!" she laughed.

"My Christmas present? Since when do we get each other Christmas presents?" They usually picked out something together.

She just laughed at him. "See you soon. Good bye!" She hung up before he could question her further. Her tone of gaiety contrasted so greatly with the fears he had entertained the night before that he had to smile to himself. At last it was beginning to seem like Christmas to him.

Not long after that he found Emma on his doorstep when he answered the bell. "Come in," he invited. "How did you find me?"

"Oh no, I have to get back to the hospital, thank you. I looked you up in the phone book so I could bring you something by way of thanks." She handed him a wrapped gift. "I hope you like it. I never asked you much about yourself, so I'm making a wild guess. Do you like science fiction?"

Gareth laughed. "Since you've given away the contents of your gift, I'll tell you right away that I love science fiction! I once aspired to write it but it's been years since I've even gotten a rejection letter." He wondered at her merry smile, which seemed prompted by something other than what he had said.

"Enjoy your Christmas! As my grandmother says, nothing is a coincidence! She and I wish you a very Merry Christmas!" She ran down the path toward her car and waved. Gareth waved back and wished her grandmother a speedy recovery.

He was happy that her mood had brightened, but somewhat in a mystery as to why. He should have asked her more about her grandmother, but she was already driving away.

Gareth was still thinking about it when Beth came home. It was so good to see her that for a few minutes all he could do was hold her tightly against him and enjoy the feeling of her soft brown curls on his neck and the motions of her breathing. Here was one human being he never grew tired of, who always had beautiful sensations to offer him and whose happiness meant more to him than his own.

He noticed right away something different in her manner. She seemed more mysterious, more gentle, more feminine than ever, even while she reeled off all the news about her business trip. *Whatever* it was, it was pleasant. He enjoyed it.

After dinner, when he least expected it, she said casually, "I have a Christmas present for you." She said nothing further.

"Well...?" he said.

"Well what?" she replied.

"Are you going to give it to me?"

"No," she said.

"What?"

"It's not wrapped, like a proper gift," she explained.

"Do you want me to discreetly go downstairs for awhile?" Do you have to get it out of the car, or what?"

"No," she said.

"Where is it? Can I have it now or is it for later? Let me see it!"

"You may not see it."

"I'd like to know how I'm going to receive this gift if I may not see it. Is it invisible? Where is it?"

"Oh, I have it on me, but I'm not going to show it to you just yet."

"All right," he said. "Go ahead and wrap it then. If you wait much longer it won't be Christmas any more."

"I'm definitely not going to wrap it."

"Okay, then give it to me now," he said agreeably. She was trying very hard not to smile, that much was clear.

"I'm definitely not going to give it to you now," she said.

"Why not? What kind of a Christmas present is this?"

"It's not ready yet," she replied.

"Oh, well in that case I'd rather just have you come sit on my lap and tease me about this alleged Christmas present later." She complied but remained silent. "Are you trying to tell me," he guessed, "that you are my present?"

"No. Definitely not."

"This present seems very indefinite to me in spite of all your 'definitelys.' What are you going to do to get this present ready?"

"It's really not difficult at all."

"Is it being readied in your imagination, by any chance?"

"Not at all."

"Will it be ready before bed time?"

"No."

"When?"

"In something slightly less than nine months."

She now broke out in her full smile.

Joy rushed through him. He pictured the house as he had ten years ago with a young presence, toys, cries and laughter, and more children to follow. Fulfillment of just this one wish made his life one hundred times more valuable to him. How could this be? He looked at his wife, who was looking at him and fully aware of what it meant to him. His wife—the bearer of these tidings, the bearer of new life, the bearer of his happiness. And he had almost assumed that she didn't care about having children any longer.

It was not until the next day that Gareth remembered Emma's visit. Beth found the gift on a table where he had left it and asked him about it. He explained the whole story to her while he opened the gift. As he had expected, it was a new science fiction novel.

"Aren't you going to open the card?" asked Beth.

"I didn't even see it," he said.

Beth opened the card and read the message from Emma aloud. "Dear Gareth, I swear to you that what you will soon receive in the mail was sent before I met you. I *knew* I had seen your name somewhere. I wanted to tell you right away but I thought it would be better if it remained a surprise for you to share with your wife upon her return. Thank you for all your help. Love, Emma."

"I wonder what it is?" Beth commented. "Maybe you won a sweepstakes."

"Not possible. I haven't entered any. I don't know what could top the gift I have already received," he said as he drew Beth closer to him.

Two days later he was opening his mail in the evening after dinner. He came across a letter from Carroll Publishing. He opened it rapidly and didn't bother to pick up the piece of paper that fell out of it and fluttered to the floor. "Probably some special offer coupon or something," he thought.

He glanced at the closing of the letter and saw it was from Emma Runick of Carroll Publishing. He read the letter and by the time he finished his hands were trembling. He slowly picked up the piece of paper that had fluttered to the floor. Yes, there it was. A check for one thousand dollars. The letter explained that Carroll Publishing had recently acquired *Sci-Fiction Addiction* magazine and found hundreds of unread manuscripts backlogged in their offices. A check was enclosed to purchase first serial rights to the story he had submitted three years ago. Waves of wonder rolled over him and were just subsiding when Beth appeared at the doorway.

He shared the news with her and she was extremely happy but not nearly as surprised as he. "It was bound to happen," she declared. He embraced her and his unborn child, still holding his first letter of acceptance as an author.

"Merry Christmas!" said Beth, for all the world as if she had planned the whole thing ten years ago.

"You'd think a man in this day and age would have the decency not to pretend he was in nineteenth century England, finding a pregnant woman in an office building to be distasteful," said Beth to Gareth.

"Did he say he was offended?" asked Gareth.

"Not in so many words," she replied, "but perhaps it was the way he nervously jerked his eyes to the other side of the room when I noticed he was looking at my abdomen. Or it could have been his curt order to his junior to get me a chair on the other side of the table so that I would be seated and out of his sight. No, maybe it was just the way the corners of his mouth were tightening downward—you know, the aristocratic lemon-in-the-mouth look—from the moment I entered the room. Actually, though, I wasn't sure until he said to me, 'Do you have any idea when Mr. Brooks might arrive? I appreciate your being here, and stenographers are always welcome, but I was assured that Mr. Brooks would be here in person to discuss our needs at this time.'"

Gareth laughed at her imitation. "And what did you say then?"

"I excused myself for having misled him by introducing myself as Beth. I told him I was Mr. Elizabeth Brooks, but that I more correctly go by Ms. Brooks. Do you know he actually blushed? He didn't see the humor in it, though."

"I hope you weren't too mean to him!" said Gareth, amused.

"No, no," Beth assured him. "I could see he was entirely wrapped up in worrying about his company. And his lack of humor had no small part in that, by the way; but I'm telling you this because I want to thank you for your brilliant idea of making business cards for E. Brooks. I would never have believed how much fun it would be to surprise people who were expecting a man. Who would have thought there were so many people who haven't noticed that times have changed? I'm probably also getting clients that I might not have otherwise because they would have refused to talk to a woman. This guy, for instance, has had a really rough time communicating to me. I think it will work out well for him in the end, if he can realize somewhere along the line that women are people, too. I can't quite put my finger on it, but he seems to be laboring through some fixed ideas along the lines of 'women can emote but not think,' and 'women don't even want to know anything about business,' and 'women act out of love, not logic.' I was dying to know his background—he must be at least sixty-five years old—and I finally got a question in edgewise yesterday for the first time. Of course he didn't want to answer it and he questioned my motives for asking, but he finally told me that he grew up in Kentucky. Do you know that he doesn't realize that some of the most brilliant employees he has are women? He still thinks women are only being stenographers and receptionists. It's a good thing he doesn't inspect the personnel department enough to start giving orders. One of the biggest trouble spots in his company is a department where he's got a male employee who is acting out of jealousy and spite and making poor decisions. I'm trying to find the right way to explain the whole thing to him."

"Is he willing to fire employees?" asked Gareth.

"Yes," Beth replied. "He'd have no second thoughts about letting anyone go who broke important company policy. But spite and jealousy aren't mentioned anywhere in company policy. And they are feminine traits, not masculine, as far as he is concerned. I don't think this individual will need to be fired, however, so I don't expect to be proposing that solution, or even encouraging it if by some remote chance it is mentioned."

Beth had hung her jacket up, slipped off her shoes, and stopped talking to look at the day's mail. "We have an invitation, Gareth! It's from Cecilia Whitney. What quaint handwriting. Isn't she Emma's grandmother?"

"That's right," said Gareth. "What has she invited us to?"

Beth read through the note quickly. "To her house. For tea. I don't think I've ever received a private invitation to tea. At least not since I was a very little girl."

Gareth and Beth arrived at Cecilia's house together the following Sunday afternoon for tea.

"Come in, come in," said Cecilia when she opened the door. "Snap and pop, now. We don't want to let the air conditioning out." Beth smiled at Gareth as they hurried on through the doorway so Cecilia could close the door. Mid-July was not a comfortable time and their last wish was to stay any longer than necessary out of the range of air conditioning. Especially Beth, who was expecting her first child in the next six weeks.

The house was simple but full of things that had obviously been part of Cecilia's life for some time. Gareth had been here only once last December when he had responded to Cecilia's accidental phone call to him during her stroke. He hadn't gone inside her house, and though he'd seen Cecilia's granddaughter, Emma, several times since December, he had not seen Cecilia. She looked better than she had that evening, but still not long for this world, as Emma had told them.

"Do you like plain tea?" asked Cecilia. "I know they've got fancier teas these days than we ever had when I was young. I just drink plain tea. That's all I have, so if you don't like it you're welcome to have a cup of hot water instead." She spoke with her back to them as she walked into the kitchen slowly, shuffling as if in pain.

"Plain tea is just fine," said Beth. "Would you like me to help you?" Beth walked into the kitchen.

"Twenty years ago, even five years ago I wouldn't have let you do it, but I've lost my pride," said Cecilia. "No, I haven't *really*. I suppose I simply don't want to drop the blasted tea cups on the floor, which I'm afraid I might do with these weak hands. Honestly, getting old is the most preposterous thing anyone ever invented."

"I agree," said Beth.

"Now don't go thinking I brought you here to listen to all my complaints," said Cecilia.

"Oh no—" began Beth, before Cecilia interrupted her.

"I want to talk to you about the baby. I'm sure you've given it much thought, but it's likely you haven't heard the things I'm going to tell you."

Gareth peered into the kitchen, surprised that Cecilia was even aware that they were having a baby. She hadn't mentioned it in the invitation. Cecilia's slow-moving body was such a distraction to her and everyone else that it was easy to forget there was a very sentient being in charge of it.

"Don't look so surprised," she said to Gareth. "Nothing is a coincidence. Just remember that. I get so confounded tired of these airheads going around today saying 'What a coincidence!' Coincidence, my foot. They like the idea so much they made a cliché out of it. Horse feathers. Sit down. You're making my hip hurt, standing there like that."

Gareth sat down and watched Cecilia shuffle over to the easy chair and carefully sit down. Beth came out and quietly asked her a question about what she wanted to serve with the tea.

"Honest to Pete, I can't remember," said Cecilia. "Look in the cupboards and see what I have. Appreciate it, dear. It's really not important. What's important is—oh, *no.* I forgot the notebook."

She started to arrange herself into a getting-up position but Gareth said, "Can I fetch something for you?"

"That *would* be much faster, wouldn't it," Cecilia mumbled. "Take a look on my desk and see if there's a blank notebook. I *intended* to have this all written for you, but I couldn't read my own writing, much less expect you to read it, so I'm afraid I'm going to have to ask you to take notes while I give it to you verbally."

Gareth went down the hall in the direction she pointed and looked for a room with a desk. He found it, and after a quick search through a couple of drawers he also found a pen. He brought these to the living room table and set them down, just as Beth was setting down a tray of assorted scones, rolls and muffins, followed immediately by steaming cups of plain tea.

"You children go ahead and drink your tea and I'll start my talk," said Cecilia. "I don't know when I might run out of steam, so I'll be as fast and brief as I can. First a question. Do you have a name picked out for the babe?"

"We've narrowed it down to several," said Beth. "Melody, Sherrisse or Camille."

"Ahhh," said Cecilia. "I like Camille. But what if it's a boy?"

"Modern science tells us it's a girl," said Gareth.

"Hmmph," said Cecilia. "She should probably be named Camille. But check it with her when the time comes and see if she likes it."

"Good idea," said Beth.

"Oh, and write that down," Cecilia said to Gareth. "Go on. Humor an old woman. I want you to have this all in writing. This is important."

"Will do," he said as he picked up the notebook and started.

"Let me tell you briefly what's important, in this order. Write this down. Warm, no frightening noises, not hungry, clean diaper, something pleasant to look at, something pleasant to listen to, stories."

"Stories?" said Beth.

"Even babes like to be read to. Don't underestimate babes. People think they don't understand anything because they can't say anything. Not true. They get bored to tears, just like anyone else. Oh, and no baby talk please."

"They don't like it?" asked Gareth.

"Maybe some do, but I don't, do you?" said Cecilia.

"Don't know as if I remember that far back," said Gareth, "but I'm not prone to baby talk anyway."

"As to Christmas," said Cecilia, "remember one important thing: music. Standing in line to sit on Santa's lap is *not* the thing. Presents are not really it either, unless they have music in them. Concerts, records, whatever confounded devices they have for playing music these days, just have music and lots of it. Old music and new music. Everything from *Coventry Carol* to *Chestnuts Roasting*. Forget the silly toys, I'm telling you. If you don't have fine Christmas music you're going to have an unhappy girl."

"But why music?" asked Beth.

"Simple," said Cecilia. "The child is going to be a poet and needs to hear music, that's why. When she is a bit older and can read, it will be books. Don't let her have a lack of either one."

Gareth and Beth exchanged interested looks, and Gareth wrote furiously in his own shorthand style to get it all down on paper. Cecilia went on for the next fifteen minutes, giving them detailed instructions on feeding, clothing and providing instruction for the child. Out of respect they listened attentively and Gareth captured it all on paper.

Finally he had to ask. "I appreciate this advice, and I have recorded it all. But I have to know why you've been so kind as to give it to us."

Cecilia looked at him strangely and said simply, "Isn't it obvious?"

Gareth and Beth were still trying to realize what she was talking about when she said, "Well, run along now. I think I've run out of steam. You keep that notebook, you hear me? You keep it and make sure it's near when you've got that newborn crying in your ear. I don't often extract promises out of people, but I'd like you to promise me that."

"Done, Mrs. Whitney," said Beth. "I promise we will keep it and consult it."

"Thank you," she said, accepting Beth's pledge as true.

Two weeks later Gareth and Beth attended Cecilia Whitney's funeral. Emma approached them afterwards and said, "Grandmother asked me, right before she died, to make sure you have the notebook. Do you know what she meant?"

"Yes," said Gareth, and he told Emma briefly about the tea, mentioning that Cecilia had requested that he take notes on how to care for the child they were expecting.

"That sounds just like grandmother," said Emma. "I wouldn't be surprised if that notebook is a lifesaver for you. I don't know how it could be, and I don't know what grandmother was thinking, but I can only advise you not to be surprised at anything."

They went home that evening and read through the notes. Beth continued reading books on childbirth and child care, as she had been doing for months, but she also often reviewed the notes from Cecilia during the next three weeks.

On August 26, Beth's water broke and her doctor advised a C-section due to various factors. The next morning Camille Brooks was delivered surgically and pronounced healthy. Camille was cleaned up, wrapped in a receiving blanket and handed to Beth. Gareth was beside himself with joy.

"She *does* look like a Camille, doesn't she?" he said to his wife.

"I have to say that she does," admitted Beth. "Look how calm she is. She's not crying or fussing at all. I'm very glad to have you, Camille," she said to her newborn. Camille looked calmly into her eyes.

Several weeks after returning home from the hospital, Gareth was unable to stop Camille's crying. She'd just been fed and changed. Even picking her up and rocking her did not help.

Beth picked up the notebook on her nightstand and looked at it. "Is she warm enough?" she asked Gareth.

"She's wrapped up in her blanket, so I think so."

"Are there any frightening noises?" Beth asked.

"Nothing new. Just us talking."

"Okay. We know she's fed and changed. How about showing her something pleasant to look at?"

"Are you trying to say my face is not pleasant?" he said.

"How do I know what she finds pleasant?" said Beth. "Try some different scenery."

"That's a bit far-fetched. Her eyes aren't even open because she's crying so hard."

"Well tell her to open them," said Beth.

"All right. I'll try anything." He brought Camille over to the kitchen and held her in front of a reflective copper pan hanging on the wall. "Take a look at this, Camille," he said to the baby. He held her so that her eyes were several inches from the pan. "Open your eyes and look at this. Do you like this color?"

Camille gradually stopped crying and opened her eyes. Gareth moved the pan so she could see how it reflected light. He walked her around to different parts of the house and showed her as many interesting things as he could find. Within half an hour she was asleep and he laid her in her cradle.

"Amazing," he said to Beth.

Nearly four months later Camille was growing and developing at least as well as expected. She had started smiling and uttering what sounds she could. Grandparents, parents, aunts and uncles were preparing to shower her with Christmas gifts because she was the long-awaited first child of the Gareth Brooks family. Beth and Gareth had learned to sing to her, play her favorite radio stations throughout the day, and read her stories. She responded well to fairy tales, science history and Shakespeare, gurgling along with the reader. If she did not like something that was read to her she fussed and cried until the reader changed to something she liked.

Emma came over on Christmas Day and brought a present for Camille. It was a book of poetry.

"I know this is premature, but I've had grandmother on my mind lately. She once said to me, 'Do you know that I didn't even know poetry existed until I was eighteen years old? That's a horrible waste. Next time I'm going to be a poet. I think it's the most worthy existence there is.' I didn't know if she was just saying it to be emphatic or if she really believed in reincarnation, or what. We never really discussed it. My family was like that. We didn't discuss things."

Gareth and Beth looked at each other. "When your grandmother had us take notes about raising the child," said Gareth, "she told us that Camille would be a poet."

"She did?!" said Emma. The three of them fell silent and looked together at baby Camille, who lay on a blanket on the floor. She gurgled happily at Emma. The three adults looked, knew who they were really looking at, and simultaneously tried very hard to pretend that they didn't know.

In the Morning

By Keenan Brookland, 2006

In the morning life is beautiful.
The sun comes through the window and the cat purrs.
Opportunities abound.

Indian Humanity

By Amit Kapoor

Humanity!
O' Humanity!
Where are thou?
Or have you from the civilizations,
Been banished?

Are you residing beneath
Some politician's chair,
Or hiding beneath
Some terrorist's beard?

Has your voice been suppressed
By some pundit's chants, loudly expressed,
Or all your gaudy elements
Been crushed by some anti-social elements?

These are some questions we have to answer,
Or prepare ourselves to suffer.
For no civilization can survive
If it can't revive
The religions of Love, Unity and fraternity—
Leaving behind distinctions
As Islam, Hinduism and Christianity!

Today,
Some of the pressing needs
Are a few good deeds
That will create creeds
Not based on any greed,

But,
Are devoid of the feelings
Of hatred or casteism,
And based on the pure feeling of
Indian Humanity.

JOY

By Slate Bender

Flame and Star

By Keenan Brookland, 2006

In the candle's flame I see a future.
I am not a fortune teller;
I am a dreamer.

I see a culture that could be.
I see a culture that others are letting exist.
They are not the same.

Will wishing on a star help to change the direction of this culture?
Why don't the leaders see what I see in this flame?
Why do they accept and forward lies to obtain office?

By this flame and by this star
I wish for a way to show my people a better world.

FOLLOW THAT STAR

By Slate Bender

The Game of Life

By Amit Kapoor

Raindrops are falling,
The clouds are dark,
The Sun is hidden,
It has no reason to laugh.

The dark clouds
Have a silver lining,
Through which the sun's rays
Come out shining.

The Game being played
Is the game of Life,
Where Sun symbolizes victory
Over clouds reflecting strife.

PASSING THOUGHTS

Perpetrated by Slate Bender, 1998-2000

Spelling bees are better for girls. The boys excel at expelling.

Sometimes the "real world" is just a "screen saver" in my daydream program. But my delete key is broken.

Real blasphemy is making less of yourself.

Not trying just a bit harder qualifies as a Spiritual Crisis (Emergency).

I think Dr. Doolittle is okay—it's Dr. DoTooMuch we need to worry about.

I thought of a good health plan. Keep my mouth shut!

When I see the way some people respond to life I can only think, "What a waste of good stress."

Snowman quote: "I've made an ice of myself."

Cat quote: "I paws for major feets."

I challenge a few ghosts to haunt the White House.

I have attempted to determine for whom the nutcracker squeaks.

Two practicing music together just duet 'til they can't stanza no more.

Report-Inn could be a theme for a coffee shop with side tables for attaché cases, for businessmen on the run.

Diane Riseagain could be a pen name for a reincarnationist.

Rib hugging denims could be marketed as Belly Jeans.

Baggy Plus Britches could be called Elepants.

Government motto: We roll out the red tape for you.

When you consider that The News is a business rather than a service, you can shift your viewpoint of it.

All persons considering entering the field of Psychiatry should be given a free Introductory Lobotomy with follow up electric shock treatment and daily cocktails of addictive mind-altering drugs so that they might experience firsthand the effectiveness of the technology in their field.

Indian name for slow starter: Running Bee-hind.

With all the creative fashion designers in the world, why can't one think of something to replace neckties??

I think the Texas Two Step originated when someone saw a cowboy trying to stamp some cowpie off one of his boots.

Is your life best summed up by nouns, verbs, adjectives, or punctuation?

I've been shaking this darn bottle for days on end because it said "Shake Well." How do you know when to stop?

Have you ever asked the morning, "How do you dew?"

How about chaining up some cafes which show local art? They'd be "Gallery Galleys," featuring local artists and cuisine.

I told my niece, "I'm a real 'unk."

How about a new bargain store chain called "Cheapo Depot"?

Psychiatrist dance music: Shrink Rap.

Interesting Possibilities for Book Titles:

Tales From the Skeptic Tank by O. Pinion.

Diary of Siamese Sheep by Mutton Jeff

Siesta Music by King Naptune

Greener Grasses by R.U. Sertin

Throne to the Loins by P. Pot

A prisoner of one's own imagination or a prisoner when away from it? Your call.

I'm just having a hot air day.

The Wall

By Amit Kapoor

There's a wall between you and me.
As-hard-as Rock; as-soft-as air,
Penetrable-as-water and hurting-as-life.
You don't understand me—
I don't understand you.
But we both love each other—
I hear dust falling between invisible wall.

The wall is our ego which we don't let go.
Let's discuss our problems.
Let us sit down, holding hands
Beside the pool near the bonfire;
Let us be swept off by the waves of passion.
Perhaps the wall will melt,
And there would be no more dust around.

Romance, How to Avoid

By Keenan Brookland, 2009

The title of this essay is misleading, because no matter how many techniques I have practiced in romance avoidance, none of them has ever worked for very long. So when I run across people who feel hopeless about ever finding romance, I am always puzzled. Maybe such people will find this information helpful.

In spite of the name Keenan, my gender is female. The boys always thought of me as one of them, though, from the time I hit the baseball over their heads on the first try.

In the beginning I practiced all-out pursuit rather than avoidance, but it was unsuccessful. There was a game called Kissing Bugs played by my childhood friends and me. The game consisted of girls chasing boys around the lawn. Any boy caught would be kissed. The front lawn was the play zone, and the parking strip lawn was the free zone, so a boy could not be caught if he jumped over the sidewalk to rest in the free zone for a few seconds. I was very fast and able to catch all of the boys—except Greg, who was the object of my affections. So when he had a "time out" to tie his shoe, I thought I would just sneak in a kiss out of sheer admiration. His reaction was anger because I had cheated, much to my dismay.

Later I told my friend across the street that I loved Greg and wanted to marry him, but she reported this to her mother in front of me and I got the idea that I was committing an indiscretion or weirdness of some sort by having such an idea at the age of 8. I didn't talk to anyone about it after that.

Somewhat after that we had a Batman and Robin neighborhood fan club, and our affections were all transferred to Robin. We expressed our feelings in subtle ways of our own invention, such as kissing the TV screen when Robin appeared on it and making up new romantic lyrics to tunes we knew. I think one of them began, "Got to catch my Robin, wrap him up in my arms."

In fifth grade someone told me "Paul likes you." I must not have understood what to do about it, because for lack of any other ideas on how to behave, I made fun of him to my friends. I blush to think about that now, as he was a very nice boy. He asked me to play marbles with him one day at recess when it was the craze, and I declined out of embarrassment.

In sixth grade I took a fancy to a Mexican boy named Henry because I thought he was quite cute. I told my friend across the street about this. It seemed safe, because she had told me she liked someone. I didn't mention—or even think about—love or marriage, so I was within the bounds of socially acceptable behavior for my age bracket. Then she wrote "Keenan + Henry" on the post that held up the roof over their front porch, to my amazement and humiliation. Not once, but multiple times in huge letters. I realized I had erred again.

Around that time I became aware—thanks to some friendly neighborhood boys who said so—that I was ugly. So, I avoided talking with boys as much as humanly possible. I did not attend any school dances until Eighth Grade Graduation. All my friends were going to this dance and I was not going to be able to gracefully escape attending. I really wasn't too sure if anyone would ask me to dance. But I hadn't been there long when the boyfriend of someone in my circle of friends asked me to dance. It turned out to be a slow dance, and I felt the whole time that I was betraying my friend. Fortunately I lived through it, but I decided never to go to a dance again.

I never did go to another dance, until I changed my mind. I always reserve the right to change my mind about anything I have decided.

In tenth grade I worshipped one of my teachers, and this was a pleasant way to avoid romance, as well as being perfectly safe. But then he moved away and I wrote him letters, as did a number of other students, to whom he was equally inspirational. This kept me busy for the better portion of a year.

Then I had to wear a dress to school for a singing performance, and after that a boy in the math class started calling me. Out of politeness I listened to what he had to say, which was not much. I struggled vainly to try to understand what he was attempting to communicate to me, because all that he ever seemed to discuss was trivia. And I mean trivial trivia, such as opening a drawer and telling me what was in it. He did have a sense of humor though, which I appreciated.

He was known as one of the "hoods" who frequented the back parking lot to smoke, and I didn't take his attention seriously. He mentioned at one point that he felt he needed a good Christian girl to reform him, and I took that with a grain of salt too. It did not ring very true.

I eventually accepted an invitation to go meet him where he was staying for the weekend to "learn how to play the guitar" one evening. I don't know what I expected, but after a cursory few strums on the guitar and a game of pool, he ended up playing soft rock music on the stereo and sitting very close to me. He verbally requested permission to make a premature overture, telling me he had never formally asked permission of a girl before and that I should be honored. So I practiced a somewhat lame method for avoiding romance by saying, "I'll think about it." Before he had worked out a strategy in answer to that, my stepfather called up and scolded me for being out late, and told me to come home immediately, so I was saved by the bell.

To my great surprise, my friend approached me the following Monday at school and said everyone in choir was talking about my nearly-romantic episode, and having a good laugh over the fact that I had said, "I'll think about it." I was more than a little angry about this. I found out that he had been working on two girls at the same time to try to get them to come over and spend time with him. When he succeeded with me, he informed the other girl without revealing my name, apparently to increase his value in her eyes. She demanded to know who it was and what happened, and he eventually ended up trading that information for the name of a person she knew who had originated a piece of slander about him.

He called me after that, and out of such ingrained politeness that I was physically incapable of slamming down the receiver on him, I spoke with him. I told him I was upset about what he had done and somehow he smoothed it over. He continued to call and eventually come over to my house. I developed some affection for him, but as he had no visible aspirations in life, I could not take him seriously. Eventually he informed me of other girls he was pursuing, perhaps in an effort to coerce some sort of response from me. He never appeared again, though I did later learn he had been gossiping to others about me.

There were a couple other romantic gestures in my direction. They made their declarations in my 11th grade high school yearbook, of all places. I do look fondly on those persons and hope they are happy. As for the fellow who played girls one against the other, may he be struck by enlightenment.

In college and the years thereafter there were a few suitors. This defied all logic. By high school I had refused to learn anything further about cooking, so according to popular theory (among some members of my family), no one should have ever wanted to marry me. And yet I discovered that there were interested parties who themselves were quite willing to do all the cooking. I was told that one male said of me in college, "it's too bad about her face," and yet there was always at least one who liked to gaze at it.

When I was in college, a somewhat older man that I had met on my job took me on a one-day business trip with him. He seemed personable enough, and carried on an intelligent conversation about his possessions (such as a twin-engine plane), millions of dollars of business deals he had accomplished, and various conservative opinions of one kind or another. The words sounded all right, but at no time did I feel as if we were really communicating. I couldn't seem to gain any real insight into him. He was following a formula of some sort that I did not understand. That was the last time I saw him. I only learned much later that there is a stratum of businessmen who search for college girls, some of whom are only too happy to exchange their attentions for a few additional amenities in life, and long-term support through college in some cases, regardless of the marital status of their benefactor.

Note that this essay does not cover all of my own inappropriate romantic gestures, which are touched on more in another essay entitled "Uses for Tuba Cases."

With no fashionable beauty, with almost no domestic skills, paying no attention to clothing except to disguise as much shape and form with it as possible, cultivating a mode as low-key as I could make it, I wonder why I was unable to avoid romance?

I can only think of one logical answer. The one thing I really like to do is communicate. That is not the same as talking. Talking is what some people do to fill the airwaves with a comfortable buzz, the way I would put on a soft, warm jacket to stay comfortably warm. Complaints, gossip, telling the same jokes over and over, narratives that leave you in mystery because the same slang or vulgar slang word was used 32 times in 31 different ways, and recounting the latest TV episodes all fall somewhat short of real communication in my opinion, though they may have their place at times.

Communication has two basic requirements from my point of view, and one of those is thinking up something to communicate beyond social responses. The other requirement is a person on the other end who is really listening or looking with a desire to know what the first person thought.

Communication is a fun activity, whether it is a silly expression exchanged across a room for comic relief or a deep discussion of the eternal mysteries. My husband and I always laugh at those classic moments in a story when one character says to another, "We will not speak of it again." Certainly the novel would resolve much sooner if they would speak about it. But of course misunderstandings, regrets, irresistible and unspeakable longings, creeping hidden resentments, and all sorts of other poisonous things can develop in the absence of thorough communication. If you love anguish and melodrama in your own life, don't communicate!

A chemistry professor once told a story that many years earlier he had accidentally splashed a toxic chemical in his eye and was thrashing so wildly that his wife had to sit on him to hold him down sufficiently so that she could wash out his eye. That's the philosophy I have on getting someone to communicate. If you have to sit on them to keep them from squirming out of it, and hold a big stick in the air as motivation, it would be better than letting them not communicate. I don't know how some people manage to go years and years without knowing what their closest associates think and do. Apparently there is a time-honored philosophy that when people are upset or sulky you should just leave them alone until they come out of it. Or that asking them nicely once and receiving no answer or a brush-off is sufficient reason to give up asking.

Once, when my son was very young, I had to ask him at least twenty-five times what he was upset about. He was extremely upset and would not tell me why. Maybe you have experienced yourself the sensation of being so upset that you literally can't talk temporarily. What I had to do was ask my son yes-or-no questions that he could reply to with a shake or nod of the head. I took his point of view as best I could and guessed repeatedly as to why he might be upset, and when I finally got very close he started talking about it. Just at that point another person in the room—the person whose action had upset him—piped up and began ridiculing him for feeling that way, so it took considerable skill to keep this communication going forward. I had to try to quiet down the other person while continuing to get my son to speak.

It can be hard to admit to someone that you are upset if you consider you should not feel that way about it. My philosophy is that it's best to just talk about it, because while you hold it in and continue to be ashamed of feeling that way, it continues to tie you up in knots. Once you get it out in the open, you are the master of it and it usually evaporates. It didn't appear to be the philosophy in the household where I grew up—I remember being told many times, "If you can't say something nice, don't say anything at all." I got sent to my room if I violated that. The reductio ad absurdum is that eventually one just goes to one's room and never comes out. When I was in high school, family complained that I stayed in my room too much. I had accumulated too many things I couldn't say.

It took some living and learning for me to arrive at a different conclusion. There are considerate ways to say what one is feeling; and just because you are feeling that way doesn't mean you have to believe it is correct or intellectually valid.

Then there is the factor of a person becoming upset because he misunderstood or could never figure out what someone else said or meant. This is the basis for many situation comedies. In my own life, occasionally my husband will use too many pronouns in what he is saying and I haven't the vaguest idea what he is talking about. It can take a few minutes to clarify conversations at times, because I have to trace back all the things he's assumed I know that he is referring to before I begin to understand what he is talking about. At other times he shifts the topic in his mind without the spoken words ever giving a clue to this. I can sympathize. I have made some interesting typos when my fingers lagged behind my thoughts, even at fast typing speed. Talking with someone whose mind leaps ahead of his mouth can be like talking with a crossword puzzle, and although I'm not particularly a fan of crossword puzzles, I do very much like talking with my husband. Sometimes the originality of his thoughts is staggering. But I like this. I definitely never wanted a wind-up husband who daily said, "I love you, dear" on cue, smoothly hiding all his real thoughts and ambitions; or worse, failing to have any.

One of my core beliefs is that people are always interesting when they are really communicating. But in my rash youth I was sometimes wrapped around a telephone pole by my own opinions about the opinions of others.

I remember meeting someone in college who freely confessed that he had tried to be voted best-dressed in high school. My initial reaction was shock that he felt no shame over such a materialistic, self-centered goal. But are we not all trying to get attention and impress, delight, or amuse others in our own way? The only sin would be to insist that you get all the attention and never give any to others. And some people really do create a work of art in the way they dress. I marvel at it now. Whenever I look in my closet I always feel like I have nothing presentable to wear so I just wear something comfortable and sit in the back.

One girl in college said she determined who she would date based on whether he drove a cool car. I thought she must have been joking, but she continued on in all seriousness. If anything, I would have crossed cool car owners off my list as insufficiently spiritual, or at least regarded them with suspicion. But for all I know her method of selecting men was far better than some of my early methods. And come to think of it, I remember how much affection I felt for the first car I owned back in 1976, even though it was not much to look at. I learned how to change its oil and tires, adjust the timing, and jump-start it (out of necessity, unfortunately).

I find that the more alive I feel, the more I want to communicate. And the more I communicate, the better I feel, provided understanding is achieved. At the end of the day I believe that this attitude not only invites romance of the best kind while discouraging the worst kind, but also makes possible a stable and happy relationship of any sort.

THE SNOW COUPLE

By Slate Bender

Love

By Amit Kapoor

Prayed for—
Craved for—
Eulogized—
Received—
Enjoyed—
Used—
And then—
Deposed.

A Friend

By Amit Kapoor

The cool umbrella, the shelter it gives,
The weather it faces, the life it lives—
Reminds one of a friend, so hard to find,
One amongst thousands, a rare piece of its kind.

He protects you from the heat,
He warms you through the cold,
His mere presence is a treat,
That brings joys tenfold.

Slowly She Walks

By Keenan Brookland, 2006

The girl was walking slowly.
I watched her for many minutes.

She was in another world
that did not seem to be very pleasant for her.

She did not notice the warmth of the sun
or the fragrant lilacs overhead.
The birds sang but she heard only crying in her depths.

I presented her with a small token of the beauty around us.
After a few moments she realized I was there.
I urged her to take the flower. She reached for it and held it.

She looked confused, as if kindness and beauty were
incomprehensible.
So they are, in certain worlds.

I gestured to the beauty around us, inviting her to look.
My smile fell on her pale cheeks without a return smile,
But slowly she began to warm. She looked at the tree.

She smiled hesitantly.

Jo-Seppy

By Kendall Roman, 1998

Rita Henley heard her mother scolding her. She had been singing a tune to herself in the bathroom while she was taking a bath. It was a song she had learned at school:

> "My paddle's keen and bright,
> flashing with silver,
> Follow the wild goose flight,
> Dip, dip and swing...."

She loved the thought of paddling in a canoe, and the line "flashing with silver" sent her into long minutes of imagining.

Rita's mother had what she called delicate nerves. Rita and her father had to be very careful not to bring on one of her migraines with careless activity.

Mrs. Henley's face appeared at the bathroom door. Her breathing was heavy after hefting her two-hundred-eighty pound frame across the room. "Rita Henley! Awful girl! Stop that right now!" This speech drained her. She groaned and turned back toward the living room couch, mumbling to herself about how God had cursed her with the noisiest of children. Rita finished her bath quickly by washing and rinsing her fine, long blond hair and drying off. She went into her room to read one of her favorite books.

Some day, she promised herself, she would sing as much as she wanted, all the time, in grand buildings. She couldn't understand why her mother hated her singing. It was backwards. Other mothers would come to school concerts and clap at the end. They seemed very happy to hear their children sing.

Rita's father liked to hear her sing. He was a sad man who sometimes drank too much beer, but he would always come to the school concerts. Rita knew he liked her, though he spoke little. He almost looked happy when he sat in the audience at school and heard the school chorus sing. Rita would see his face light up while they were singing, but after the concert he looked like he was going to cry and wouldn't say anything. Rita would ask, "Did you like it,

Dad?" and he would nod for a long time and smile, but he still looked like was going to cry.

Rita read part of her book, *Charlotte's Web*, and finally lay down and fell asleep. She had dreams of singing to huge crowds of people in faraway lands, but she couldn't remember much about it in the morning.

The next day when she walked home from school there was a moving van at the house on the corner. No one had lived there since the Hopkins family had moved out five months ago. It was slightly dilapidated, but so were most of the houses in Silverdale. It was small and rural; even the few relatively wealthy townspeople had no taste for fine houses, and the economy of Silverdale did not permit others to indulge such tastes.

Rita watched with awe as a beautiful old grand piano was wheeled out of the van and towards the house. It was taken in through the French doors in the back of the house. An elderly man hovered over the movers. This man was very worried about the piano, but the movers paid no attention to him. When they had disappeared into the house, Rita wandered home.

The next day when she walked home from school, the house on the corner was quiet. Rita was curious about the piano. She stopped and stared for a few minutes, wondering about the man and his piano. She didn't want to disturb anyone, so she quickly walked to the French doors at the back of the house and peered inside. It was hard to see inside and she saw no piano. Suddenly the man appeared from around a corner inside the house and he looked right at her. She didn't run away, though she knew she shouldn't be looking in the strange man's French doors.

His mouth moved as he said a word—though she couldn't hear what it was—and he walked toward her with a look of wonder in his eyes. He opened the French doors and said, "Hello."

"She said, "My name is Rita. I live over there." She pointed to her house.

"Oh. I see," he said. He pulled a handkerchief out of his pocket and used it to remove a few drops of moisture that had accumulated on his forehead. When he had finished with that he looked at Rita again and said, "Of course. How silly of me." He thought he had seen a young woman at first, but it was only a girl.

Rita remained there looking at him, waiting to see what he would do or say next. He gathered himself together, cleared his throat and finally said in a friendly way, "Well then, Mademoiselle, what are you doing looking into my house?"

"I wanted to see the piano," she said. "I've only seen pianos like that on TV."

"Is that so? In that case I will show it to you myself and you will see it in person. Come right in, Mademoiselle. Follow me. I'm warning you, though, pianos are to be heard and not seen."

"Oh, I know that," Rita said. "Are you going to play it?"

The man did not answer right away, but continued walking. She followed him across the room. The cream-colored paint was flaking off the walls and the carpet was worn and scattered with occasional dark stains. There was not yet much furniture in the house, but what was there was ancient. In a small alcove there was an old rolltop desk with a matching chair, and a small table that was now delicate with age. Upon it was a picture of a pleasant-looking woman. As they passed by the kitchen area she saw there was no table for dining, but a few used dishes had been hastily placed on the kitchen counter.

The old man led her around a partition to the living room, which housed only a chair and the grand piano. Several stacks of music books and manuscripts stood on the floor near the piano bench. They were stacked in such a careless way that it looked as if they might fall over any minute, or perhaps someone had just been sorting through them.

"Mademoiselle," the old man said as he bowed stiffly and indicated that she should be seated in the chair. It was comfortable and Rita settled down into her seat, fascinated with the old man.

Every other stick of furniture in the house was slightly dusty, worn or rickety, but the piano was polished to a beautiful shine and every key was perfect. The old man sat down with great ceremony and turned to his audience.

"Mademoiselle, what is your pleasure? Mozart, Beethoven, Brahms?"

Rita sat right up and said, "Can you play the kind of music they play in a big, big house, right before the lady comes out and sings?"

"Ah!" he said grandly. "Opera."

He played the overture to Mozart's The Magic Flute. Rita was delighted and could not help but dance around the piano. After they finished, Rita clapped her hands and laughed.

"Do you sing?" asked the man.

"I sing in the fifth grade chorus at school," she said proudly.

"Yes, that's all very well. That is not what I mean by singing. Would you like to be my pupil? I will teach you to sing as they sing in the big houses." He stared out the window for a moment and Rita had to touch his sleeve to get his attention.

"What do they sing in the big houses?" Rita asked.

"Oh, excuse me, Mademoiselle. Sometimes I wonder if I am dreaming.. What do they sing in the big houses? Well, they sing opera. Mozart wrote some of the best—"

"Who is Mozart?" interrupted Rita.

"Mozart was—he's been dead about 200 years, you know—a brilliant composer. He wrote for Royalty. But let's begin your instruction. Sing a scale for me. Begin here." He played a chord on the piano.

"What?" She laughed.

"Take a good breath and sing along with the piano. Just sing 'Ahhh.'"

She did so as he played each note. She stumbled a little bit at first, but she got it. He praised her efforts and had her keep repeating it until she could do it perfectly and easily. She smiled brightly.

"Very well done, Mademoiselle!" he exclaimed. Such a clear and pretty voice, too. We are going to go far with you."

Rita beamed for a moment. Her sparkle faded abruptly with some private thought.

"What is it, Mademoiselle?" inquired the man.

She was reluctant to speak, but finally said, "I can't."

"Oh, I know I'm supposed to be retired and so forth, but we can always make an exception. Besides, I think this will do me good. Really, you must say yes."

"My mother won't let me."

"But why on earth not?!" exclaimed the man, genuinely surprised.

"My mother said I couldn't take ballet or join Girl Scouts or any of the things my friends do because we can't afford it. My father doesn't earn very much money," she explained miserably.

The man considered this at length. He would have been quite happy to collect no money at all for the lessons, but he didn't want to run into difficulties with her parents. He envisioned people of low income being insulted by offers of charity.

"What if we were to work out an exchange of sorts," he began. "Perhaps you could give me lessons in exchange for the lessons I give you."

"But what can I teach you?" she replied in disbelief.

He opened his mouth to speak as if the answer were obvious, then realized after a few moments that it was not. He finally asked, "What do you know how to do?"

"I can make cookies," she said.

"Cookies." He lagged in the unexpectedness of it for just a moment, then launched into the subject with enthusiasm. "Oh, excellent! I had just been thinking I would like to have some good, homemade cookies and really did not know how I was going to get them. I would rather eat cardboard than those dry things they sell in the store." He made a face. "Do you really know how to make cookies? This is my lucky day! I place myself in your hands on this matter."

Rita was smiling at his antics. When he finished, she grabbed his hand and pulled him into the kitchen. "Where do you keep your flour?" she asked.

The man looked puzzled. "I confess I have none. Is that what you use to make cookies?"

"Yes, silly," she said. "I'm going to have to show you how to do shopping first."

She found out he didn't even have a recipe book, so she ran home and got hers. She showed him how to find the recipe and make a shopping list from it. By the time they got all the ingredients listed for chocolate chip cookies, it was time for Rita to go home.

As she ran out the door Rita waved and said, "Good-bye Jo-seppy!" It sounded so natural that at first Joseph did not realize what she had said. As she disappeared from sight, it struck him. He had never told her his name. Nor had anyone used that pet name for him since—but surely there was some logical explanation for it. He would ask Rita tomorrow and that would be that.

Rita, breathing quickly, slipped into her chair at the dinner table just as her mother was beginning to fret to herself about all the trouble it was to keep track of her daughter. She lay on the sofa in the den with her feet up and a look of pain on her puffy face.

"Why is it so hard to keep that child under control? She's never here for dinner on time and always makes me worry. Where does she go off to? Why is she so hateful that she does this to me?"

"Mom, I'm in here," said Rita from the dining room.

Rita heard muttering from the sofa. Her father had finished preparing dinner and went to help her mother to the table. They usually had dinner around 7:30 because her father worked until 6:00 and then had to come home and fix dinner.

The dinner, the evening, the whole world seemed wonderful to Rita as she thought about her new friend. He had said she sang well! It was so exciting she wanted to jump up and dance around, but she was afraid it would upset her mother. She knew by instinct not to mention anything about it at the dinner table. Anything she liked was usually condemned as a nuisance to her mother, so she said nothing.

The next day she went to the man's house after school, but this time he was sitting in a chair waiting for her by the French doors.

He watched her and noticed with a pang that she approached with some caution, as if she were used to rebuffs in life, even if not ultimately discouraged by them.

He thought he had been tired of life when he retired several months ago, but this girl revived something in him. He had spent forty years teaching music at the University and, bitter as it was to him, had no major credits to his name. The genuinely talented students had seemed to be fewer and fewer as years went by, and he detested the moral laxness of his fellow department members. Some went to pot parties with the students or had love affairs with them. He felt he had little in common with them, was hopelessly outdated in his ideals and tastes, and tired of trying to write a great opera while distracted by professorial duties. His life seemed wasted.

Rita reminded him of one student who had not been a waste: Marie. She would have been an exquisite performer, and perhaps he could have written for her the Opera that he had always dreamed of writing. She had died suddenly of meningitis before she graduated, and his hopes had somehow died as well. If Fate could be so unjust, why hope for anything from life?

How strange that Fate should deliver this girl to his doorstep. He had decided to be a recluse of sorts and discourage all visitors. He wanted only to end his days in the purity of study of the Masters. He had no family ties, no friends. The appearance of Rita, however, was surprisingly welcome to him, and he found himself being as lighthearted as he had once been when he still had his dreams.

Rita stopped a few feet from the French doors and waited expectantly. Joseph smiled and gestured for her to let herself in. She lost all reserve at that point and bounded in joyfully, stopping abruptly in front of him as if checking all movement until he gave her permission to resume.

"Mademoiselle, so nice to see you again," he said as he rose and bowed.

Rita beamed, did a little curtsey that turned into a twirl, and then landed in an even prettier curtsey, laughing.

Joseph straightened and said with dignity, "It is an honor to be your teacher". He led her into the piano room.

Rita took a position near the piano and said, "I feel like I know you better than anyone, and I just met you."

Joseph was arrested by the simplicity of this statement and emerged from his light-hearted facade to address her as directly as she had addressed him. "I did mean to ask you why you called me Jo-Seppy yesterday when you left."

"Did I?" she asked. "I don't remember that. I'm sorry if I called you the wrong name. What is your name?"

Wondering now if his memory had failed him, he reverted to the amusing air he found it so easy to assume for her. "Well, let me think. I often forget it this early in the week. Don't look at me as if you don't believe me! After so many years of living I have a great many things to remember and I don't rate my own name among the most important. I do, however, keep my calling card for occasions such as this."

He gave her a card and she said, "Oh, it's Joseph, like in the story of Joseph and Mary in Bethlehem." This unexpected association jarred him, especially since it reminded him of Marie.

"When I am teaching you, it would be proper for you to address me as Mr. Steinman, but at other times you may address me as you wish."

"Where did the name Jo-Seppy come from?"

"There was someone who called me that once."

"Why?"

"It was a variation of my own first name and similar to that of a famous composer I admired greatly. His name was Guiseppe Verdi."

"Oh." She began thumbing through some of the music on the table nearby. Joseph watched her closely. She was only ten years old and knew next to nothing about music, yet she scanned the titles and opened the books with the facility of one quite familiar with the contents. "Oh look—this one says Mozart," she observed. "Would you play it for me?"

"I will. And will you sing it for me?"

Rita laughed. "Yes!" she cried, and then added, "But you'll have to help me."

He sat down to play what she had chosen. It was "Non Mi Dir," an aria from the opera *Don Giovanni*, which she had found in a collection of soprano arias.

"These words don't make sense, Joseph," she said, looking closely at the pages.

Joseph turned to her confidentially and said, "That's because Mademoiselle has not yet studied the Italian language. It's a very beautiful language and one you will find well suited to singing."

Rita nodded to herself. "I thought maybe that was another language. We have learned a little bit of Spanish in school but it doesn't look like this. What language is 'Mademoiselle'? I meant to ask you before and forgot. I like it when you call me Mademoiselle, though, because it reminds me of ladies in very pretty long dresses that puff way out, and their hair goes up to here and falls down in curls all around. Is that what it means?"

Joseph nodded. "More or less. For you and me that is a perfectly good definition."

Rita laughed. "You are so funny, Joseph. You are the only person who calls me something instead of my name."

"It's much more fun isn't it?

She considered it for a moment. "Well, yes, I think it is." She turned her attention back to the music she had selected. "Play it now, Joseph; I mean, Mr. Steinman," she directed.

He began the introduction and was transported to another culture, another time, another language—the language of music, of drama. These were more vivid to him than the everyday life that others cherished. He could not help remembering the lessons with Marie as well. To his surprise, he began to re-experience emotions he had felt twelve years ago. He had to remind himself that this was a music lesson. There is no room in a music lesson for personal emotions. There is only the emotion created by the music and with the music.

Joseph was pleased at how well he was doing with this young student. His youngest student prior to this had been sixteen and already trained in music theory. Rita had plenty of ability and was quick to learn. She duplicated even the difficult passages if he slowed them down for her. He played the ending with a flourish and she clapped.

"This is fun," she declared.

"How right you are, Mademoiselle," said Joseph. Rita threw her arms around him playfully and then darted off in a little dance around the piano. Joseph smiled and daydreamed.

"Joseph!"

Rita had wandered off into the kitchen and came running back at full speed right to his side.

"You didn't do your dishes!"

"I knew there was something I'd forgotten," he admitted.

"But I told you that you should do them right away when they are easy to do. It's much harder if you wait."

"You are absolutely right, Mademoiselle," he said. "I remember your telling me that yesterday, very clearly. But I failed to mention to you that I don't know how to do dishes. That was something I always hired housekeepers to do. I know that it has to do with soap and water, but that's the extent of my knowledge. Is it very complicated?"

"Oh no, not at all. I've had plenty of practice because I do most of the dishes at my house. I can show you how."

"Very good, then."

"Do you have children?" she asked.

He was slightly taken aback at the abrupt change of topic. "No, Mademoiselle. My life has been a life of music. I have created many children of music. I have raised young souls from newborn abilities to masters of their art, and I have written or arranged some of their music as well. This left me no time to marry and have children."

"At least maybe you could afford to have decent things, then. My mother always says that she can't have anything decent like new furniture or dresses because it costs so much to raise me. Is that your wife?" she asked, referring to a photograph she had held behind her back and now showed him. It was the photograph from the alcove near the desk.

"Oh no, Mademoiselle. She is someone I admired greatly once." He could not help it; his eyes misted over at the memory, assisted by the poignancy of seeing Marie's photograph in Rita's small hand.

Rita looked closely into his eyes. "Are you crying?" she asked.

Joseph paused a few seconds to make certain he was in command of himself. He fully felt the irony of being in this position in front of a young student; he, who considered that emotion was something to create in others and not to experience himself. He stood up, and in the act of semi-formally bowing to her he regained some of his sense of self-dignity. "With all due respect," he said," I see that you have not yet been taught to be polite."

"I'm sorry," she said immediately. "I—"

"Don't apologize," he continued, and settled back into his seat. "After forty years in a world of false politeness I have learned its shortcomings. You are the first person who has ever dared to honestly inquire into my personal feelings. Not that I deserved it. I haven't made anyone else's feelings my business. I had my idea of what I should be and how I should conduct myself, and whenever someone tried to approach me I would not let them. For many years this served me well and I worked in the field of music simply for the pleasure of my accomplishments. But then everything changed."

"How?" asked Rita, since he failed to explain.

"Well, the lady whose photograph you now hold. There was a quality about her—" and he attempted to put it into words in his mind but then recalled he was speaking to a ten-year-old girl whom he had just met.

Before he could gain control of the conversation, Rita spoke up. "Did you love her?"

The question made him raise his brows, so Rita explained, "I've read about it in stories. It's okay if you tell me."

He looked at her and began to be amused. "If someone wrote a book about me I suppose that's what they would say. But that doesn't really tell the truth about it."

"What's the truth?" she queried.

Joseph smiled. "This lady was the first person who ever held my interest. I don't mean romantic interest; I mean just plain interest, as in wanting to see what she would say or do next. It was happiness itself to be around her because she was ambitious and good-natured. She was beauty in words and action to me. Others speak of bodily features when describing beauty, but Marie had more than simply a beautiful exterior. She was constantly creating beauty: in generous ideas, music, graceful motions, cheerful expressions. You can't see it in her picture. A flat piece of paper is a poor means of conveying what she was."

"I think she's pretty," said Rita. "But her face is too thin."

He laughed. "That's what she used to say. I could never convince her otherwise, much as I tried."

"That was very nice of you, Joseph," replied Rita. "You're a nice man."

"It was simply the truth as far as I was concerned. She might have been a great opera singer, but it was hard to convince her of that."

"Maybe she wanted to marry you and have children."

Joseph laughed at the absurdity of that. "I was thirty years her senior. That was impossible." He shook his head to himself and added, "I'm sure that was the furthest thing from her mind."

"Don't you read any books or newspapers? Lots of old men marry young ladies."

"Mademoiselle! What must you think of me!? My life is my music and I did not think of my students that way. Let other men marry them. My calling in life was to develop their musical skills to perfection and give beauty to the world."

"That's not the way it goes in the books," she reminded him.

"Your point is very well made, Mademoiselle," he smiled. "Perhaps I have not been conducting my life the way it goes in the books. I am not in agreement with my fellow man on certain points. Now I find myself retired at the young age of sixty and seeking only solitude. Of course, that was impossible once you walked into my back yard."

Rita asked, "Is that good or bad?"

He smiled warmly. "How can it be other than good? Now let's get on with our lessons."

Three weeks passed in this way, with Rita making steady progress in her voice lessons and Joseph learning how to do his dishes and laundry and make various kinds of cookies. Rita always managed to make it home in time for dinner, but one day her mother fell ill with bronchitis and instead of napping through the afternoon she worked herself into a fury because Rita was not there to wait on her.

"Rita, I want to know what trouble you've been up to. It's just not right for a girl to be missing from 3:30 to 7:30. What were you doing? I won't have my child involved in criminal activities instead of doing something constructive. You sit right here and tell me what you've been doing or I'll have your father take his belt to you."

Rita's mother glared at her while she slowly sat down and tried to think of something to say. If she told the truth her mother would find something wrong with it and forbid it. "I've been playing with my friend," said Rita.

"Playing!" roared her mother. "I've been sick in bed and you've been playing? What kind of a selfish brat are you? Rita Henley, you are not to do anything but come straight home from school from now on. That's final. Now bring me another pillow and my heating pad before I get one of my headaches."

Rita sat numbly at the dinner table afterwards. Her happiness had ended abruptly and she hadn't much hope of restoring it. She contemplated simply disobeying, but she couldn't see how that could go on for very long. Her father had "taken his belt to her" before, so she didn't fear that. He was too kind to strike her and they had simply moved out of her mother's sight and pretended to do the deed to make her happy. How could one do that day after day, though? Wouldn't something worse end up happening?

She fiddled with some carrots on her plate and ignored her tuna casserole. Her father, who rarely said anything, finally spoke up and said, "You feeling okay, Rita?"

"Yes, I'm fine, Daddy," she lied. "I'm just not too hungry right now. May I be excused?"

He put his hand on her forehead and exclaimed, "Oh no, you've got a terrible fever! Let's get you to bed right away before your mother catches something from you." He picked her up and carried her to her room without any protest on her part. She didn't have a fever, so she wasn't sure why he was doing this.

He laid her gently on her bed and said, "Don't mind your mother. She don't mean it. You don't have to stop playing when she gets sick. We'll figure out something." He stopped when he noticed that Rita was crying.

"It's not that Daddy, but thank you anyway," she said as she clung to him.

"It'll be all right, you'll see," he said. His absolute wish for her happiness made it impossible for her to continue crying.

"If I have to come home straight from school every day it will not be all right. I don't know what I'm going to do, " she said.

Rita's father frowned and said, "When your mother makes up her mind it's hard to get around it without upsetting her too much." He fretted silently with the problem for a few moments and then asked her, "Do you suppose you can go a few days not playing with your friends and see if she cools down?"

"But Daddy, I wasn't playing with friends. That's just what I told Mom." She went over to the little box on the dresser in which she kept her treasures and removed the business card that Joseph had given her. She handed it to her father and said, "This is the man who moved into the Hopkins' old place. He is teaching me how to sing and I am teaching him little things I know so that you and mom won't have to pay. You know how much I love singing, Daddy. When I go to Joseph's house I can sing as much and as loud as I want. If I can't ever go there again I will be so sad, Daddy."

Rita's father reached for her and assured her that they would work it out somehow. He slipped the card into his pocket.

The next day he worked over his lunch hour so that he could leave work early and stop at Joseph Steinman's house on his way home. Joseph was relieved to find out the reason for Rita's sudden disappearance, though not pleased about it. The two men discussed the situation and decided they would try to get her excused from a portion of the school day in order to continue her lessons. Joseph wrote up a paper for Rita's father to take to school, attaching one of his cards and praising Rita's talent profusely. Rita's father thanked him many times and headed home to give his little girl the good news.

When he walked in, his wife was wailing and crying, "George! Please help me. I'm dying, I'm in terrible pain."

He went to her side to comfort her and carry out her orders. This happened at least five times a year, so he was used to the routine. The Doctors never found any but simple ailments in her, yet she was always sure that she was going to die. All he could do was hold her hand, soothe her, give her what she asked and call the hospital and doctor for advice. Inwardly he rebelled this time because he wanted so to give Rita the good news as soon as she walked in the door. He felt it was not right of him to resent his wife's illness and tried as best he could to change his attitude.

Joseph considered the complications of the situation. In the three weeks since he had begun with Rita his hopes had not been disappointed. Here was musicality he had not seen since Marie. Starting this young she was sure to outgrow him within a few years, but he would have had his hand in the making of a great singer. His dream was alive again. The one flaw in it was the mother. Rita's father had not precisely stated it, but Joseph sensed that the mother was not in favor of Rita's music lessons. Sometimes these family matters can be fatal to a career, he thought. He profoundly wished that all such obstacles would dissolve for Rita. As if his life were meant to culminate in her success, he aligned every fiber of his being with her dreams to sing.

Lost in reflection, he did not hear the siren until it was quite loud and stopped suddenly. He wondered if there were a fire in the neighborhood, but a brief glance out the living room window did not reveal any smoke. He went back to his desk and planned the course of Rita's lessons for the next two years. He consulted books he had not opened for years on voice method and teaching. He would do the best job for Rita that he could.

Joseph was not yet done with his planning when he was interrupted by a knock at the door. It was Rita and her father. He was just about to greet them enthusiastically when he noticed their air of seriousness and anxiety. Had her father had second thoughts? Joseph prepared himself for an hour of persuasion, if the need arose, and invited them in. They stepped in but

Rita's father declined to sit down and took a deep breath as he chose his words.

"I was wondering, sir, if you wouldn't mind watching Rita for a few hours. Her mother is .... quite ill and has gone to the hospital. I'm going to go there now and wait. I'm sorry to trouble you but I was hoping you wouldn't mind it for a few hours."

"Of course not!" replied Joseph. "I hope your wife will soon recover. Do they know what is wrong with her?"

Rita's father looked reluctant to answer. "Well....it's pretty serious." He saw that Rita had walked off to the piano room so he stepped closer to Joseph and lowered his voice to a whisper. "Heart failure." He swallowed uncomfortably and looked at the floor. Joseph was unsure of the man's sentiments.

"I'm so sorry. I hope all comes out well. I will be glad to help in any way I can. Don't worry about a thing."

"Thank you, thank you," Rita's father mumbled, and took his leave.

Rita had gone to the piano room but sat gravely on the bench, looking wistfully at the keys. Words escaped him, so he continued to simply observe her. He did not know what to say to a young girl in real danger of losing her mother.

Rita sighed and began to pick out notes on the piano. Joseph went to his alcove and sat silently listening to her. In a few minutes she came to him and asked, "Does it hurt to die?"

"I don't know," he answered. "I have heard many people speculate about it, and it may be that it doesn't hurt at all."

Rita thought for a few moments and then said, "Maybe it will be better for my mother to die, because she is always feeling nervous or sick."

Joseph said nothing. Rita seemed to display no grief at the thought, nor any ill will toward her mother. Very level-headed of her, thought Joseph.

"I'm tired," Rita said.

Joseph prepared his own bed for her, as it was the only one in the house, and saw that she was comfortable before settling into his most comfortable chair for the night.

Some time much later, he got up and went to his bedroom. Marie was in his bed. She heard his approach and smiled up at him sleepily, holding out her hand. He vaguely remembered that Marie could not possibly be here, but he was tired enough that the whole matter was slightly confused. She sat up when he did not come over, and reached for him. He was oppressed with guilt; apparently he had been living some other life while Marie was his wife and she had been waiting for him all this time. She did not reproach him, but she kept reaching for him. He placed his hand in hers and held it warmly. He became conscious of her form under the blanket and joined her in the bed. She smiled, and as he began to embrace her she transformed into Rita. He was horrified, and quickly left the bed.

A few moments later he awoke in the chair and it dawned on him with considerable relief that he had been dreaming. He heard a knock on the door and realized that someone had been knocking for some time and this is what had woken him. He eased his stiff body out of the chair and went to the door as quickly as he could.

As he expected, it was Rita's father.

"Come in, Mr. Henley," Joseph managed to say. "Would you like some coffee?"

"No, no thanks. I just came to pick up Rita. I suppose she's sleeping." Joseph studied him carefully. He did not look grief-stricken, nor relieved. If anything, he seemed disoriented.

"How is your wife?," Joseph ventured.

Mr. Henley took his fingers out of his belt loops and began struggling with his collar, very ill at ease. Joseph didn't expect the bluntness with which he then spoke. "Dead on arrival. Couldn't do nothing for her."

After a few moments of dead silence, Joseph heard himself say, "I'm so sorry. Is there anything I can do to help?"

This offer seemed to rouse the man somewhat out of his confusion. He was able, for the first time that evening, to sustain a look into Joseph's eyes for more than one second. His speech was difficult, but sincere beyond question.

"If you wouldn't mind, it would mean a lot to me if you kept up the lessons with Rita. I always knew she was meant for that but I didn't know how to do anything about it."

"It would be my honor to continue teaching Rita," replied Joseph. They quietly parted, and Mr. Henley carried his daughter home to her own bed.

The funeral was mercifully brief and the weather appropriately gloomy. Joseph had made himself present from beginning to end for Rita and her father, George, in case they needed help or comfort of any kind. It was a capacity he had never filled for anyone before. He would have been at a loss, perhaps, if words of comfort were required, but the major support he contributed was in the handling of administrative details such as filling out forms. Rita at ten years old was more literate than her father.

There were few in attendance at the funeral. George's parents flew out, and one of his brothers attended with his wife, but Mrs. Henley's parents were long since deceased. Several of George's friends from work were present. The chapel was small and musty; it mattered little as there were no lengthy eulogies. The atmosphere of the small crowd was subdued but notably lacking in grief.

As Joseph said farewell to Rita and George for the evening, all were in a quiet mood. George thanked him and asked him what he might do in return for the kindness.

"If you have a spare one, and it's not too much trouble, I would love to have a photograph of Rita for my little music studio. Just an old custom of my students," he explained. "They knew I didn't have a family, so one of them gave me her own picture to place in my office. Over the years there were many others who followed suit and I eventually came to have quite a collection." He paused as he remembered how bitterly he had packed those pictures away at his retirement, thinking he had failed them all by permitting his life come to nothing in his own eyes. "Rita is my only student now, but she may be my most important one. Very talented girl, she is."

George's eyes lit with hope, even through the strain and dark circles that recent events had traced on his features. "I saved all her pictures," he replied. "You can have your choice. I'll show you."

Joseph followed him into the bedroom he must have shared with his wife and watched as George produced a ladder from the closet and climbed into the attic through a small access panel. He handed down a box to Joseph after a bit of rummaging. "Go ahead and look. I'll come back in a minute after I tuck in Rita."

"Thank you," Joseph said with mild surprise. Strange place to store pictures. Most parents had them out on display or in easily accessible photo albums.

He brought the box into the living room and sat down to look through it. There were very few photos in the box, and all were school pictures, kindergarten through fifth grade. No family photos at all. The sheets of wallet size prints were intact; not a single one had been cut out and sent.

Joseph looked through them, finding Rita in each of her class pictures and studying her 8x10 portraits carefully. He finally chose one that looked as if it were taken a year or two ago, but which captured the look he had seen in her when she first danced to the music of Mozart around his piano.

"Do you mind if I take this one?" he asked George when he appeared.

"It's yours," he said. "I thought you'd pick that one."

"Why?"

"It's my favorite. That's how she looks when she sings," he answered.

"Oh," stammered Joseph. "I couldn't possibly take it from you then." He set it back in the box but George immediately picked it up and pushed it back at him.

"No, I insist. I have all these others, see?" He indicated the 5X7 and wallet size photos of the same pose.

"Pardon my asking," said Joseph, "but is there some reason you kept them in the attic instead of displaying them?"

George looked sheepish but finally said, "My wife suffered so. It upset her to spend money on anything besides her medicines. I—she didn't know about the pictures." Joseph studied the man's thin frame and realized that more than photographs had been sacrificed. A wave of admiration swept over him at the thought of the quiet, uncomplaining patience of George's life.

"I see," said Joseph. "It's a pity. But on the other hand, there is nothing to stop you—that is, once a respectable period of mourning has been completed, you might consider framing some of them."

George looked doubtful.

"It may be," added Joseph gently, "that what troubled her spirit in life is no longer troubling her now. But there's plenty of time to see what the future brings. I'll be getting on home, and we'll plan on resuming Rita's lessons in two weeks. Will that be all right?" asked Joseph.

"Yes, that will be fine," answered George, smiling and no longer doubtful. "I thank you very much." He shook Joseph's hand and the two parted, with Joseph's admonishment that George was to let him know at any time, day or night, if help was needed.

The next day Joseph rose early and procured a frame for his new photograph of Rita. He carefully stored Marie's photograph; not in the box where he had thrown the others, but in a drawer by itself. He felt that he should concentrate all of his attention on Rita, his only student now.

A shock of nervousness ran through him as he thought of the responsibility he was undertaking. Here was someone who wanted to go the full route, to be a great singer, and it was in his hands to make her one. Or at least to start her properly on the route and make sure she ended up with the right teacher and agent.

"What am I thinking?" he asked himself frantically. "I am so out of touch with such things. Not to mention that I know *nothing* about children!" He got into his car and started driving to the city. There was no doubt in his mind as to exactly where to go and who to see about the matter at hand.

Three hours and a couple of coffee stops later he drove into the familiar parking lot of the University. He walked straight to the music library and there was Mrs. Lattimore, predictably repairing and maintaining old manuscripts with the air of one who obviously considered them precious. Mrs. Lattimore, the music librarian, had seen decades of music students through their degrees, helping them with research assignments and repertoire searches. In Joseph's private opinion, she knew more than most of the music professors, especially since she aspired to no status or recognition, but just loved to help and absorb knowledge herself while she worked. It was well known, besides, that she had four grown children and close to a dozen grandchildren. She had always struck Joseph as the maternal type, and other women seemed to admire her accomplishments in the realm of child-rearing.

"Good afternoon my dear Mrs. Lattimore!" he said cordially to attract her attention, bowing slightly in her direction when she looked up.

"Well, if it isn't Dr. Steinman! I never thought to see you here again. How are you?"

"A good deal stiff in the nether regions after a long drive, to tell the truth," he replied.

Mrs. Lattimore smiled. "It'll do you good, then to show this young man around the campus." Joseph noticed with some irritation that there was indeed a young man stationed near her, looking expectant. "I'd do it myself but of course I can't leave the library unattended."

Mrs. Lattimore finished with the manuscript she had been repairing and placed it on a neat stack in a box labeled "To be shelved."

"This Gregory Devault. He is a high school senior, touring various colleges before making his choice. He will be double majoring in French and Music. Gregory, I would like to present Dr. Joseph Steinman, a very distinguished professor who taught here for forty years."

"A pleasure," said Gregory, shaking Joseph's hand.

"Indeed," replied Joseph. "I would be happy to show you around as soon as I finish one piece of business with Mrs. Lattimore. Will you excuse us for a moment, please?" He took Mrs. Lattimore into the back room as Gregory obligingly turned to look at something else.

"Dr. Steinman, are you all right?" asked Mrs. Lattimore, concern and puzzlement in her eyes. Joseph wondered if he looked so driven as to be alarming.

"Yes, yes, of course. But I do need a good, long bit of advice from someone trustworthy. Would you do me the honor of having dinner with me this evening and hearing my predicament?"

Mrs. Lattimore's eyes widened. "I hope it's nothing seriously dreadful," she said. This was not the aloof and intellectual Dr. Steinman that she had known.

"No, nothing like that. I apologize for being cryptic, but I will explain it to you fully when we have a chance to sit down. Would that be all right?"

"I suppose so," she replied hesitantly. "I'll just have to call Gerald and let him know he's on his own for dinner."

"Oh, how silly of me. I don't want to deprive your husband of your company. Why don't you invite him along? Do you think he'd mind?"

"Much as he claims to like my cooking, I've never seen the man turn down an opportunity to eat out. I'm sure he'd be delighted. He can't eat shellfish, but other than that he's game for anything that doesn't walk off the plate."

"Good, then," said Joseph. "I'll meet you here at 5:00—that's your quitting time, isn't it?—and then we'll pick up Gerald and head to Darby's. Would that suit you?"

"Sounds wonderful! We've enjoyed it when we've been there before," replied Mrs. Lattimore.

Joseph carried out his tour duty, not with pleasure, but painlessly. He had just the glimmering of hope that he was no longer trapped in the dead-ended feeling his life had assumed in this place. Consequently it looked more attractive to him. Sensations that fell just short of memories crept into his awareness; inklings of a much younger Dr. Steinman with a lifetime of imagined achievement ahead of him.

While waiting for his dinner appointment, he visited the University Bookstore, then drove across town to the sheet music store. Rita should have her own books. He mulled over the choices for half an hour before he selected three books for young singers. Then it was time for dinner.

Darby's was rather crowded, even early in the evening. It was more popular with professors and parents than with the college kids, so was a good choice. Joseph asked for a booth in a quiet corner, or the nearest thing to it they could manage. The waitress was surprised to see him, remembering him as a long time customer but rumored to have become a recluse, living far away, after he retired.

"Hey Doc, whatcha doin' back here?" she asked.

"A man can stand only so much of his own cooking," he said good-naturedly.

"Get tired of peanut butter and jelly sandwiches?"

"Oh, I never prepared anything that fancy. Pretzels and beer were my staples, but when I was feeling especially culinary I would open a can of sardines," said Joseph.

"You never touch a drop of spirits, Doc. Don't lead these nice people astray! He always ate his vegetables, too," she said to the Lattimores. "Well look at him! That's not the figure of a beer and pretzel man."

"This lady hopes for a good tip from me, obviously," said Joseph.

"You bet I do," she said. "And if you'll let these nice people order, Doc, I'll prove I deserve it!"

Joseph gestured to the Lattimores to proceed with their order.

The meal went well, the Lattimores being pleasantly amused at a side of Dr. Steinman they had not seen before. Joseph explained how he met Rita, what progress they had made so far, and the very recent death of her mother.

"It sounds like you're doing very well with her so far," commented Mrs. Lattimore. "What possible advice could you need from me?"

"Things *have* gone well," Joseph admitted, "but there are so many factors I know nothing about. She is a just a child, and I know nothing of what to expect as she goes through her years of... uh... development. She has just lost her mother, and her father is a semi-literate laborer. Granted, he has been quite encouraging so far, but he has no idea of the path ahead of his daughter, if she is to travel it fully. What if he starts to put on the brakes when he begins to realize? What if she grows up and gets married *instead*? What if some of these blasted psychological factors they prattle on about go awry because she isn't having a normal childhood with a mother and regular childhood activities, and so on?"

Joseph ran his hands through his hair and sighed.

When he looked up, Mrs. Lattimore gave him a kindly smile. "First of all, Dr. Steinman, I want to remind you that you needn't worry about all of these things right this moment. You do have plenty of time to handle things as they come up."

"Perhaps, but I would of course like as much of a head start as possible," said Joseph. "I would be grateful for anything you can tell me about your experience with children, and what you know about how to make a performing artist who won't crack under the pressures of life."

"I suppose I can do that," Mrs. Lattimore said. "We'll start with the child aspect of it." Mr. Lattimore ordered a second brandy, knowing Mrs. Lattimore would be too occupied to notice.

"From all my years of observing children," Mrs. Lattimore continued, "there are really only two basic kinds. By that I mean the two extremes, but of course there are many degrees of in-between as well. There are children who know their own mind and are constantly busy working toward a purpose, and then there are those children who don't know their own mind and just wander aimlessly or stir up trouble. If you have the first kind, the best thing is to let the child get on with it. Help him when he needs help, correct him when he is erring badly, and give encouragement when needed, but basically *don't interfere with that great driving force behind his own purpose!* And don't mistake the swiftness with which some children cause trouble to be a driving force behind a purpose. I mean a *constructive* purpose.

"The second kind of child is the one that takes more effort to raise. These children need more than just instruction. They need a large amount of direction, and sometimes constant supervision as well. They can't hold their attention on one thing for long, they can't think of anything to do and prefer to be entertained, they cause trouble to get attention. Punishing them savagely never works. Threatening savage punishments doesn't work, either. Rewards don't particularly work by themselves; at least not for long. And drugging them is downright criminal, in my opinion. The only thing that works is good firm direction. They must be directed and made to get up, get dressed, get bathed, eat the food, read the book, play the game, say hello and thank you; ignoring any of their backtalk or horseplay rather than getting mad at it or answering it. Of course every child needs to be told things initially, but some children just have a rough time getting the hang of doing things on their own.

"I've seen parents who barely survived their own childhoods (because they were such troublemakers) turn around and treat their children with all the restrictions and punishments that *they* should have had, when in reality their child may not need them at all.

"In short, you just have to notice what you're dealing with in the child before you. You must judge how much freedom is needed and how much direction is needed for that specific child. There's no other way to be right," she concluded.

"I do know what we're dealing with in Rita," said Joseph. "She is the first type; no question about it."

"I agree," smiled Mrs. Lattimore. "But I also wanted to add that dealing with a child of the second type is no reason to give up hope. With enough good direction, a child—or even a late-blooming adult, for that matter!—will snap out of his dormancy and take charge of his life with purpose. Do you know that sometimes very purposeful and alert children have raised the adults in their lives when necessary?"

Joseph had a strange sensation that she was somehow referring to him, but he brushed it aside. She couldn't possibly have any idea about me, he thought.

"Let me clarify what you mean by freedom, Mrs. Lattimore," said Joseph, clearing his throat. "I don't allow students to have lessons whenever they want, to sing difficult pieces before they know how to read music, to practice less than the minimum required, and so on. I don't see that I should treat Rita any differently."

"Very true, Dr. Steinman," said Mrs. Lattimore. "She will probably do best if you treat her much as you do your older students, taking into account that her means and stamina might not be as great as they will be in the future. With a child there is a delicate balance between not crushing their wildest dreams with long explanations of the grueling road ahead and guiding them sensibly down the path in such a way that they always feel they are accomplishing something.

"Did you not say you let Rita sing Non Mi Dir almost the first day?" asked Mrs. Lattimore.

"I did do that, yes," replied Joseph.

"I gather that is not how you start your older students?" said Mrs. Lattimore.

"No; but then my older students have some background in music besides 5th grade chorus, have probably heard symphonies and operas before, at least in music appreciation class. This child is living in a backwoods town where the highest form of entertainment is drinking at the tavern—"

"I know some very literate and cultured people who live in the backwoods," interjected Mrs. Lattimore, "but I see what you mean. Her mother was a tyrant, her father is semi-literate. And yet—"

"And yet she precociously walked into my studio, picked up a book of arias, turned to Non Mi Dir and requested that I play it. My other students do not do such things!" answered Joseph.

"No," she said musing to herself for a moment. "Quite a joy to be around a child like that, isn't it?"

"Emphatically so! I thought I didn't care for children. If they were all this pleasant I would have to change my mind about that. Dreadful thought, isn't it?"

"Dreadful? But why?" said Mrs. Lattimore, surprised.

"A confirmed bachelor must have and hold his reasons for being in that state until death does part him from them. I would have to question my own judgment if I were to develop some affinity for the idea of having children about the house."

"Worse things have happened than a change of heart, you must admit," she replied lightly.

"Regret is near the top of *my* black list, almost as annoying as needles in the derrière. Of course I can always take refuge in Alzheimer's Disease, if necessary. Isn't that right, Mr. Lattimore?"

Mr. Lattimore, whose thick trifocals had slipped slightly further down his nose with each sip of brandy, raised his head and eyebrows with a valiant lurch and peered at them through his lenses.

"Balderdash!" he said dramatically.

"My point exactly," said Joseph as the three of them laughed.

"One of Gerald's great virtues is that he doesn't take life too seriously," said Mrs. Lattimore. "As to his vices—"

"I'm too lenient with my wife," he said, and she slapped him playfully on the knee.

"Would either of you care for another drink or a dessert menu?" asked Joseph.

"No, thank you, Dr. Steinman," said Mrs. Lattimore. "But I did want to briefly answer your other question."

"Oh heavens, did I have another question?" he said, puzzling.

"How to make a performer who will not crack under pressure?" she reminded him.

"Yes! Please tell," Joseph said.

"I've thought about that one some," Mrs. Lattimore began. "In a nutshell, though, I would recommend three things. One, make sure she keeps performing and always has a realistic short term goal to work toward. Two, make sure she *never* gets into drugs. I mean street drugs, uppers, downers, happy pills—anything along those lines whether "prescribed" or not. Three, make sure she learns to choose her people well and takes critics with a grain of salt. As long as she has at least one true supporter, such as her father, and *you*, she will probably be fine. Simple, no?"

"No! But it does *seem* so after the brandy, doesn't it?"

The three of them left Darby's together and Joseph drank some strong coffee at the Lattimores' home before starting the long drive back. He had altogether enjoyed himself and contemplated Mrs. Lattimore's advice all the way home. He fell into bed when he arrived home at 11:00 p.m. and slept soundly.

"Is there a woodpecker in here?" he mumbled crossly to himself as he lumbered stiffly across the floor to fetch his robe the next morning. He'd been hearing tapping for a minute or so. Ignoring it was not working, and further sleep was now impossible.

He walked out into the hallway and could hear that the tapping was coming from the French doors. Rounding the corner he saw Rita's blond hair and large eyes looking at him through the French doors. She broke out into smiles and jumped with excitement when she saw him.

"You're home, Joseph!" she cried through the transparent door.

Dressed in his robe, hair standing on end and the signs of slumber heavy in his eyes, he hesitated.

"Are you okay, Joseph?" she said, or at least he thought he heard those muffled words through the glass.

He had no choice but to let her in, though it did nothing for his personal dignity to be seen at that hour.

"You weren't home when I came for my lesson yesterday," Rita began, "and I thought you were mad at me, or you went away, or something. What happened?"

"Mademoiselle, I'm afraid I can't understand English or any other language until I've had my morning coffee. Would you care to join me?"

"I don't drink coffee, Joseph, but I know how to make it. Where is your coffee maker?" said Rita.

"Oh, I don't have one of those contraptions," he answered. At least I don't think I do, though there *are* some unpacked boxes still in the spare bedroom."

"That's impossible," she said matter-of-factly. "You must have a coffee maker if you make your morning coffee. I'm sure you can remember where it is, if you think for a moment. Or should I look for it? That would be fun!" She ran off into the kitchen and began opening cupboards.

Joseph began to wake up a little and strolled into the kitchen. "Let me explain, Mademoiselle. Not to interrupt your fun, of course, but you won't find a coffee maker anywhere in this kitchen. My jar of instant coffee is right here." He opened the cupboard next to the sink and pulled out the only thing in it besides salt and pepper shakers, which was a jar of instant coffee.

"First thing in the morning I have one cup of this," he told her. "Then I get dressed and shave, after which preparations I am presentable enough to go downtown to Nan's Nook for a *real* cup of coffee. Would you care to join me? By Jove, I just realized that you're not in school! I knew something was out of the ordinary. You don't strike me as a girl who would play hooky. All right, Mademoiselle; what is so funny? Is my hair upside down?"

"Oh—it is!" she cried with fresh laughter, "but that's not what I was laughing about. Today is *Saturday,* Joseph." She became serious again at once and added, "But maybe back when you were little they had school on Saturdays. Did they?"

"Fortunately not. The trouble with me is that I don't have to remember which day is which anymore. So I don't. Which reminds me, I understood that we would begin our lessons again in two weeks, after—" he stopped short, feeling it would be insensitive to refer openly to her mother's death and the mourning period. "Didn't your father tell you?"

"Was he supposed to tell me I can't have lessons for two weeks? Why, Joseph?" she wanted to know.

"Well... I just assumed... I ... thought it would be wise.... but actually I have reconsidered and I see no reason to... Oh dear, I think I need that coffee," he muttered.

Rita laughed and said, "Coming right up!" She read the directions on the jar and started the water heating, then had Joseph sit down on the nearest chair. "Just relax and don't worry, because your coffee is on the way."

She brought the cup to Joseph when it was ready, prepared perfectly of course, and she spoke cheerfully to him as he sipped it. "Daddy and I have so much free time now that Mom has passed on. And we can do whatever we want at home. Even go to bed late! We watched the late movie last night and had popcorn. This morning Daddy made pancakes and now he's mowing the lawn. I thought I'd come check on you and I saw that your car was back in the driveway. I was so worried about you yesterday!" That made Joseph smile.

"I was doing some research yesterday, and we have some new materials to start with on Monday...if that meets with your approval, of course," he added.

"That would be perfect!" she exclaimed. "I have so much more time to practice. I even sang for Daddy at home and he clapped for me and threw imaginary roses. I told him that's what they do for really famous singers. He's a great daddy."

"I agree, Mademoiselle," Joseph said.

As he finished up his cup of coffee, Rita wandered into his bedroom. "Do you want me to lay out some clothes for you, Joseph? Oh, Joseph! Your undershirts are all sitting on top of the dresser. Didn't you like the drawer I picked out for them?"

Joseph traipsed into the little bedroom. "It was a wonderful drawer," he said, "but you know what a model of efficiency I am. I thought of all the wasted effort of putting them in the drawer when I would just be taking them out again in the very near future—but you're looking at me as if you don't believe me."

"The reason you should put them in the drawer is so that your room can be neat and you can find them. And they won't get dusty, either. I'll just put them in the drawer for you." She proceeded to do so and then paused and said, "Oh no! Look what happened!"

"What?" asked Joseph.

"You folded these all inside out. See the tag? And the seams? They should go on the inside," she said.

"Really? I can't believe that. Why would anyone want all those itchy tags and things on the inside? I've always worn mine on the outside."

"Joseph, you're teasing me!"

"Actually, Mademoiselle, though I may be making a fool of myself to admit it, I am not. And does it really make a difference, since no one sees it anyway? It is, after all, only an *under*shirt."

"I guess it doesn't really," she admitted, "but it just seems more proper to wear it the right way. So I'll fix these for you, okay?"

"I thank you very much," he said, and bowed. Rita smiled and got busy refolding the undershirts.

An hour later they were at Nan's Nook with George, whom they had picked up on the way as he had just finished mowing the lawn.

"Mr. Steinman, this is awful kind of you," said George as he sipped a hot mocha.

"Is it good, Daddy? Can I try it?" said Rita. He gave her a sip.

Joseph was astounded at the change in George. He looked a thousand years younger. Both he and Rita seemed far from depressed by the death; they actually seemed as happy and lighthearted as a couple of people could hope to be. Heaven forbid that the people in *his* vicinity should be so gladdened in the wake of his death, thought Joseph. "I'd like to propose an overall plan for the next few years of Rita's music studies," said Joseph to George.

"That sounds good," said George. Rita happily munched on a muffin and listened carefully.

"In addition to the voice lessons, I feel it would be wise for her to begin piano and music theory as well. The earlier she starts these things, the easier they will eventually be for her. She should have some practice time daily, and since you do not have a piano at your home, it would make sense for her to practice at my place. Two hours per day would be a good figure to shoot for, but if she can start with one hour and work her way up to two, that would also be fine."

Rita was doing some calculations with the aid of her fingers and said, "I can practice five and three quarters hours a day. I get home at 3:15 and my bedtime is 9:00."

"What about your dinner?" said George.

"Oh—and Joseph's lessons. I'll have to figure it all out," she concluded.

"It will be good for Rita to surround herself with examples of fine musicianship, too," continued Joseph. "I brought you a schedule of classical music broadcasts for the next month," and he slipped it out of his pocket and handed it to George at this point, "and if Rita can watch these on T.V. whenever convenient, that will add to her musical knowledge. Do you have a record player or tape player?"

"No, sir, nothin' like that. Rita's mother didn't like to hear things around the house. 'Cept men's wrestling. She'd always have me turn that on for her. Seemed to cheer her up, somehow."

That gave Joseph a jolt. He was reminded of the adage that truth is stranger than fiction. Indeed.

"We'll need to invest in something for Rita, and get her listening to recordings of music as she can. I have an idea, though, so don't worry about it for now. At the University where I used to teach they upgrade sound equipment from time to time and I may be able to pick up something they were going to throw away.

"Now, there is one other thing," added Joseph. We are helping this young lady to become a performing artist, and it is important that she does frequent performances and watches the performances of others. If you hear of any opportunities through your work connections, feel free to let me know and I will see what I can set up. I imagine that our best bets will be church services, local talent shows, women's club functions and the like."

Rita's eyes had widened and a dreamy smile hovered on her lips. "I'll do my best, sir," said George.

George was true to his word, and over the next two years Rita enjoyed almost monthly performance opportunities. She progressed well in her piano playing and began to do piano performances as well. By the time she was thirteen she had a paying job—only $30 a month, but worth far more to her than the mere money—playing piano for one of the churches. She could manage to get through the hymns, and as they didn't have anyone else in the congregation who could play, the elders of the Church voted among themselves to pool their spare money and contribute to her talent, having heard her perform beautifully in a voice so pure and true that it brought out goose bumps on the backs of their necks. If not for that, the pianist position would have been on a volunteer basis only.

One day Rita came to Joseph's house with a slight crease in her forehead. They hadn't gotten very far in the lesson before she complained of a terrible headache. She looked a bit flushed with fever as well. Her forehead was warm to the touch.

Joseph panicked. That was how it had started with Marie. She had stopped by his office one day, complaining of a headache, and had canceled her lesson for that afternoon. He heard three days later that she had been rushed to the hospital and by the time of her next weekly lesson...

"Don't panic," said Joseph. "Just—"

"I'm not panicking, I just feel—"

"—sit down for a moment while I find my car keys. I'll be right back."

"Joseph, what are you talking about! I'm just coming down with the flu. Everyone has it at school."

Joseph returned to the studio at a trot and gingerly took her by the shoulders. "Do you think you can make it out to the car, or should I call for help?"

"Joseph, I just need to get some rest, that's all. Don't look so worried. You're scaring me!"

"One mustn't take chances with this sort of thing. Let's just have it checked out. It's probably nothing, but at least then we'll know."

He escorted her to the car and drove her to the hospital, trying to calm himself and fairly oblivious to her stream of protests.

"Your hand is shaking, Joseph!" she cried when he was filling out papers at the reception desk.

"Just relax, now; everything will be fine," he said carefully.

"I think I should be saying that to you," she said.

After an hour's wait and much pacing and impatient checking at the desk, Rita was finally seen by a Doctor. After she had been examined, the Doctor spoke with him.

"Your granddaughter just has a touch of the flu. Nothing serious. She just needs rests and fluids," he said.

"How high is her temperature?" Joseph asked.

"100.4 degrees. Not bad at all. She's doing fine." The Doctor patted him reassuringly on the shoulder.

"But I've seen things like this develop into meningitis," Joseph said nervously.

"Really?" said the Doctor. "It's highly unlikely. But if it will make you feel better, I'll find a sheet of symptoms for you to take home. If she develops any of those you can bring her in for hospital observation."

"I'd appreciate that," Joseph replied.

Once he had gotten Rita home and left a copy of the symptom sheet with George, he went home and collapsed, drenched with perspiration. That he had made an utter fool of himself and looked like a doddering grandpa was the least of his worries. He'd had no idea how important Rita was to him. Was it wise to place so much value on one fragile life? Could he face going through anxiety like this again? What was the matter with him?

A couple of days later Rita was feeling much better and he went over to talk with her. She came out of her room and sat at the dining room table, still in her bedclothes and robe.

"How is my dear Teacher, today?" asked Rita, smiling. She put out her hand for him and he squeezed it warmly.

"Quite recovered, now that I see your smiling face. Thank you for taking care of yourself."

"Why did you get so upset, Jo-Seppy?" she said. She had liked Marie's nickname for him and had asked often to hear stories about Marie over the years. She called him Jo-Seppy in the moments when they were close friends, knowing she and her father were the only real friends he had here.

"I'm not sure. I didn't expect it. Believe it or not, man is not always a rational beast. I can always be counted upon to be a beast, but don't expect me to be rational."

"You think you're a beast just because you make me sing an hour of vocal exercises a day, and repeat the same passage 2,000 times?" she teased. "The *real* beast in you comes out when you do ear training. You're always trying to trick me!" she accused.

"Funny you should complain when you always call them right," he said.

"I'm just a good guesser, you know."

"Nonsense!"

"I'll prove it. I'll bet you I can guess when you're going to let me do the *Exultate*." She had heard several recordings of Mozart's *Exultate, jubilate*, full of light and showy passages and cadenzas. It had been one of Marie's favorites, and Rita liked it just as well.

"That wouldn't be hard, as I've already told you," he said.

"You call that vague phrase you used to put me off—*When your voice is ready for it*—you call that *telling* me?" she said, amused. "That didn't tell me anything. I think you're going to let me do it when I'm sixteen."

"Why sixteen?" he asked.

"That's when I will be fully developed. I read it somewhere," Rita said.

"Pardon me for contradicting you, but having a bosom does not mean that your voice is mature."

"That's *not* what I meant!" she snapped. "You're impossible!"

"Thank you."

"Jo-Seppy," she said in a different tone, after a pause.

"Yes?" he said. There was a trace of sadness in her eyes.

"I *was* upset about something that day I came with the headache. I was thinking of talking to you about it."

"Tell me," he said.

"That morning in school, Melissa came up to me at ten-minute break and said that she and Kathy and Tammy weren't my friends anymore because I thought I was so great with all my singing lessons and everything. They said I was stuck up and they weren't going to hang around with me anymore. I don't understand that. I didn't think I am stuck up. I just like to sing, and I *thought* people liked to hear it."

"They do."

"I know we've been over the fact that I'm supposed to ignore critical reviews; but I never thought that friends would turn against me just because I like to sing. Do you think I will ever have friends again, Jo-Seppy?"

"You will have thousands of friends, I'm sure of it," he answered.

"And I won't die," she said. "I promise you. I know you're afraid I might die, like she did, but I won't."

"She didn't do it on purpose," he reminded her.

"I know. But maybe she didn't have as much to live for as I do. Or she thought she didn't. Nothing could happen to me."

"Nothing except being switched by your voice teacher, young lady, if you don't get back to bed and get yourself well for your lesson on Friday!"

Rita jumped up and ran back to her bedroom, squealing, "Oh no! Good-bye, Jo-Seppy."

"Good-bye," said Joseph as he left.

For the next two years Joseph had little of consequence to interrupt his progress with Rita. There had been a couple of boyfriends wanting to come to lessons with her, which he tolerated for her sake even though next to nothing got done while Rita and boyfriend exchanged glances. Large audiences didn't seem to make her a bit nervous, but boyfriends did. She sang with only half her usual spirit and made mistakes when boyfriends were listening. Joseph gritted his teeth and said nothing, and soon the appearances of boyfriends at lessons disappeared.

One sunny April day, a couple of months before her sixteenth birthday, he decided the time was right. He invited Rita and George over for a chicken and lemonade picnic in his backyard. Rita's blond hair was now cropped, and though she had grown some it was apparent she was going to be rather on the petite side.

"I would like to announce," he said during their after-picnic round of lemonade, "that—"

He stopped abruptly and stood up, brushing the crumbs off his lap and straightening his clothing. In a more mellifluous and resounding voice he began again: "I would like to announce the debut of Rita Henley in the *University Summer Recital Series*."

"A real recital!" shouted Rita. "She had jumped up and was pirouetting about the lawn.

"Don't get so excited quite yet, Mademoiselle," said Joseph. "Let me present you with the centerpiece of your recital." He handed her a small booklet wrapped in pink tissue with gold sparkles on it.

"Jo-Seppy, you've outdone yourself!" she cried as she delicately tore the paper off. When she had unwrapped it enough to see the title, she erupted into a piercing scream of joy.

"The *Exultate!!* And I know it already, too." She began to sing it airily, flitting about the table.

"Yes, but now you're going to *work* on it."

When her mood had subsided to mere happiness she stood still and opened the booklet, reading the note in the front.

"What is a castrato, Joseph?" she asked. George raised his eyebrows. "It says here that Mozart wrote the *Exultate* for an eminent Roman *castrato*. Is that a type of nobility, or what? What is it?"

"Something that men don't like to discuss at the table. Why don't you go inside and look it up in the dictionary?" said Joseph.

"Okay." She ran in, but returned a few minutes later with the news that it was not listed in her dictionary.

Joseph looked at George, who was looking at his lap.

"Well, Rita," said Joseph, "do you notice the amazing similarity to the word *castrate*?"

Rita looked horrified. "*What??* You mean....? But *WHY* would anyone do that?"

"Money, for one thing," said Joseph. "Some castratos made phenomenal money. You have to remember, too, that several hundred years ago women were not allowed to sing in church. The high parts were sung by boys or men. It was found that a very fine quality voice could be created by castrating a man. His voice maintained its strength but the quality changed to a pure, trumpet-like tone."

"That's hideous, if you ask me," said Rita.

"I'm not arguing with you on that," said Joseph.

"This is too gross for words," brooded Rita. Suddenly a new thought struck her. "Are there still castratos singing this?"

"Good heavens, no," answered Joseph. "There hasn't been one for over a hundred years now. There are still men who sing high parts, but they are not, to my knowledge, anything but whole and healthy men using falsetto."

"All right. Then I agree to sing this piece at my recital," she declared.

"Bravo!" said Joseph.

Rita crumpled up the sparkly pink tissue paper and threw it at him.

Over the next couple of months Rita practiced daily for hours while her classmates slid into the lazy days of summer. Once she had learned to execute the notes and pronunciation of each piece perfectly, Jo-Seppy had her listen to recording after recording of accomplished artists who had performed the pieces. They made exhaustive notes on each interpretation, finally deciding exactly where Rita would take each breath and what the dynamics of each phrase would be. Rita considered each cadenza—an elaborate passage that sometimes brought pieces to a close or rest point—

and tried many different variations. Joseph was pleased that in a most instances she opted not to sing them exactly as she heard on recordings but instead devised her own. He felt he had succeeded in exposing her to enough music to give her a good ear for accepted idioms, while at the same time leaving her own inventiveness intact.

Rita's father had become quite the eligible bachelor. A number of single ladies in town who had followed some or all of Rita's many performances over the years dreamed, secretly if not openly, of being the new mother of the sparkling young girl. George was never short of volunteers for organizing recitals and performances, bringing refreshments and taking Rita to buy another new dress for her performance wardrobe. Some of them offered to buy the dresses themselves, but George would not hear of it, even if he had to slip money under their front doors which they had spent on Rita without his permission.

Several of the women were content just to be part of the bustle of Rita's small town entourage. A couple of them had grand designs on the fame and fortune that loomed in George's future with such a talented daughter. Only one had her eyes on George himself.

Genevieve Warren lived three doors down the street from the Henleys and had lived there for as long as George could remember. Genevieve had recently been widowed when George and Emily Henley moved in, fresh from their honeymoon. Each time she caught a glimpse of the newlyweds she was moved to fresh tears. Her own happy marriage had been brief and childless. She knew that the Lord had a good reason for taking John to Heaven when He did, but she had a miserable time fighting her loneliness and envy. When the Henleys had a baby girl a year later, Genevieve swallowed her feelings of self-pity and volunteered to baby-sit for them.

Emily was delighted at first, and often left little Rita in Genevieve's charge so that she could shop, visit friends or spend time alone in peace. Genevieve grew attached to the baby girl, as did the baby to her. When Emily noticed this one day, she ceased bringing Rita over to Genevieve's house and determined to keep Rita to herself, even if it drove her crazy.

Genevieve prayed daily, hoping that her feelings of disappointment and bitterness would pass. She felt punished at every turn for trying to love others, and at last she concluded that she should spend all her love on the

Lord. She doubled her prayer time, then tripled it, and joined the Women's group at church. After much prayer and consultation with the Pastor, she began helping at the Children's Hospital and volunteered to help with Meals on Wheels. Her life became so busy that she had little time to think of her losses and sorrows.

Genevieve watched as Emily Henley put on weight, grew sour and ill-tempered, and lost her prettiness. George Henley became thin and quiet, looking always halfway to exhaustion. Rita grew into a lovely blond-haired girl, but Genevieve noticed that when she tried to join the other neighborhood children in play after dinner on summer evenings, Rita would most often be summoned back to the house sharply by her mother.

"Perhaps there's something I ought to try to do for them," thought Genevieve. She devoted much prayer and meditation to the problem, but no answer came. She sighed whenever she thought of them or saw them briefly about their house on her way to meetings and charitable work. She did gather up her courage and bring some chicken soup to the Henleys once when she knew that Emily was sick, but she overheard such loud complaining from Emily at the noise made by the doorbell that she never repeated the favor. George had knocked on her door the next day to thank her again very kindly, but she still didn't feel right about it.

Emily's sudden death had been a shock, though it did make the Henleys much easier to help. George and Rita beamed whenever she brought them anything from her kitchen, and she was able to help book Rita for many performances.

News of Rita's University Recital spread rapidly and the Women's Group at church determined, upon Genevieve's suggestion, that they should hold a tea in Rita's honor and begin a scholarship fund for her. They debated for some time whether the tea ought to be held before or after her recital. Those who argued in favor of before the recital were sure that it would publicize and energize her first important performance. Those who argued in favor of after the recital felt it would be an unwanted distraction and cause the recital to be anticlimactic.

Genevieve was distressed nearly into a frenzy at the enmities springing up over the tea debate. She finally went to George one day and asked him what he thought.

"I don't know," he admitted, "but I'm sure Joseph would know what's proper."

"Oh, I don't want to bother him!" exclaimed Genevieve. "I'm sure it's not his problem."

"Well, maybe not. But like I say, he's seen a recital or two in his day and he will know how it's done. Come with me and I'll ask him. It's okay, you'll see."

She followed him to Joseph's house reluctantly and they interrupted him at work with a stack of books and manuscripts.

"Good afternoon George, Mrs. Warren. Come in. Would you like some lemonade?"

"Sure thing," said George. Genevieve nodded quietly.

"We have a question for you," said George, when they had all been seated with glasses of lemonade.

"I hope it's not a taxing one, because I've been studying this fine print for hours and I think my brain cells have all evaporated from the heat."

"Oh no, this is an easy question," said George. "The Women's Group wants to hold a tea for Rita and set up a scholarship fund for her but they aren't sure whether to hold it before or after the recital."

Joseph mopped his brow with his handkerchief and said, "Sorry, too taxing. I'm afraid I don't know why you're asking me that question."

"I'm sorry we bothered you, Dr. Steinman," said Genevieve quickly. "You're absolutely right. We'll be going now." She tried to rise to take leave, but George took her arm and kept her in her chair.

"No, no. Wait just a minute," he said to Genevieve. "Explain to him what's happening. Just what you told me."

"Oh, dear. Well, it's just human nature, you know," she stammered, embarrassed.

Joseph raised his eyebrows. "Scandalous thing, isn't it, this human nature? That's why I've opted to be a beast. But I seem to be missing the point here. What is it that's just human nature? And what does it have to do with the tea for Rita?"

"Well, you see, Donna Welch thinks we should have the tea before the recital, and Gerry Kiplinger thinks we should have it after the recital, and now most of the women have taken sides and stopped speaking to each other if they're on different sides, and they're all waiting for me to make the final decision because I'm the President and it was my idea in the first place. I don't dare say a thing to favor either side, because then they'll stop talking to me too. A few have even hinted that they'll quit coming to Women's Group if my decision is unsatisfactory. I just don't know what to do!" she ended, helplessly.

Joseph looked at her for a moment, blinking his eyes perplexedly. "I thought you ladies occupied yourselves with tea cakes, quilts and Bible verses. I had no idea you were into politics."

"They're not usually like this, but Rita is so important to Silverdale. I wish I'd kept my mouth shut about her recital and then maybe none of this would ever have happened."

"We thought you could help Jenny decide about the tea," added George, "because you know how these recitals are put on, and whether the tea goes before or after."

"Ahhhh," said Joseph. "The light bulb is going on in my dusty cavern of a head. Does someone imagine I am an authority on this subject?"

Genevieve and George nodded.

"Well, let me give you the bad news first. I know nothing about the Fourteen Thousand and Seven Rules to Etiquette in the Case of Ladies Arguing About a Tea. I don't even remember if any of my past students had a tea or not. The good news, though, is that I am absolutely sure of one thing."

"What's that?" asked George.

"You will have a handful of irate womankind no matter whether you choose before or after, even if Dr. Steinman says you should conduct it thus and so. Don't look so downcast, however, because there are two other possibilities. One is to have no tea at all. The other, and least obnoxious, is to have two teas; one before and one after. I'm sure you could alter the themes appropriately and make two acceptable events of it. What about that?"

"That might work, Dr. Steinman," said Genevieve hopefully.

"Why didn't I think of that?" said George. "Thanks, Joseph."

"Oh," added Joseph, "and get all the ladies to work on both teas, or it may just turn into a big war."

"Right," said Genevieve, "and there's still the matter of which tea to present the scholarship fund at."

"Present it to the ladies at the first one—before or after Rita is there—and present it to Rita at the second one. That will give you time to get more donations before the presentation to Rita. And invite everyone in Silverdale to the first tea, which will be here I presume?" Genevieve nodded. "Then you can invite all of Silverdale plus the University Community to the second one, and hold it right after her recital as a sort of Reception. Not as many Silverdale people will come, but certainly all the key ladies from the Women's Group will want to be there."

"Yes, yes, I think that will work," said Genevieve and she smiled at Joseph. "We'd better get busy! We have only four weeks before the recital." They departed with considerably more speed than they had come.

Genevieve presented the idea to the Women's Group the next day, and though there was a bit of confusion and argument at first, things were soon settled. The tea before the recital was to be held at Gerry Kiplinger's house, and Donna Welch was in charge of the invitation list to the second tea, which sent her imagination into new stratospheres.

Gerry stayed after the meeting was over to confide in Genevieve. "I'm so glad the tea will be at my house!" she bubbled. "It's perfect. I know George is just about to pop the question to me, so it's very appropriate. Rita will be thrilled! Most likely we can announce our engagement at the tea as well!"

Genevieve looked at her blankly, not believing her ears at first. Gerry was a 54-year-old divorcee. She didn't look her age, and certainly didn't act it, but George was only 36 and not at all a match for her. George had remained completely passive in the face of those women who had placed themselves in his path, and it was obvious to Genevieve that he was not interested in remarrying. He liked his life the way it was with his daughter receiving all the attention and praise while he helped quietly in the background.

Genevieve felt honored that he chose to seek out her advice from time to time when he had questions, and she attributed it to the safe haven of friendship that she offered, in contrast to the more ambitious single ladies of Silverdale.

"Forgive me for being surprised," Genevieve finally said to Gerry, "but I didn't know. This must be a very new development."

"Well, as I say, I just know he's got something up his sleeve. When I get a feeling like this, things generally start happening. He's so shy and it's high time he started to really live again. Besides, that girl needs a mother. She doesn't have enough feminine influence in her life, and she needs someone who can manage her through her career. Oh, Jenny—it's been so long since I was in a wedding! What do you think I ought to wear?"

"Oh, I'm sure I don't know." Genevieve's mind was a jumble of confusion, imagining Gerry as the stepmother of Rita and remembering Gerry's technique for talking with her 30-year-old daughter from her previous marriage: I just let her babble on with the phone in my ear while I do something else. I don't really pay attention to her. I've got too many other things to do.

"At least help me choose something for the tea," Gerry insisted. "You're his neighbor. Has he ever mentioned to you which dress he likes me in best? Do you know what colors he likes?"

"I could ask him, if you want," Genevieve offered.

"Oh no, that would ruin the surprise. Never mind, dear. I'll handle everything." She left Genevieve to wonder about the fate of George and Rita.

Every practice evening over the next four weeks Genevieve brought an end-of-day snack to the Henleys. During the hot weather she was sure they didn't get enough nourishing food, especially with all the excitement of the approaching recital. She brought fruit and cheese plates, fruit whips, iced drinks, cool cucumber sandwiches and festive gelatin fruit desserts. After the first time Rita ran over to share with Joseph, Genevieve decided it would be better—and more rewarding for the hero of Rita's debut, Joseph—to enlist the help of George in bringing the snacks straight over to Joseph's house when the two of them were winding up practice for the day.

"Jenny, you are wonderful!" exclaimed Rita on the Tuesday before the recital when Genevieve and George came over with a spectacular fruit plate and strawberry velvet cream. "I'll take that, Daddy. You sit down and help us eat this."

Joseph was lost in thought as the other three chatted casually. Something in the conversation snared his attention and then he heard Rita saying, "Daddy, what did Mrs. Kiplinger mean when she said I'd be seeing a lot more of her soon?"

"Don't know," he said, engrossed in strawberry velvet.

"She isn't talking about... you're not going to hire her, or have her stay with us, or anything like that, Daddy?" said Rita.

Genevieve suddenly looked extremely uncomfortable but George, his mouth full, shook his head no.

"Oh, I'm glad. She's too silly. She treats me like a stuffed animal."

"You give her too much encouragement, Mademoiselle, by stuffing yourself with dainties," said Joseph as Rita ate the first of a handful of dates.

"Just because you don't need to eat, monsieur, doesn't mean the rest of us are immortal statues. Here now, Jo-Seppy; you need some fattening up." She handed him a dish of strawberry velvet and a spoon.

"Mademoiselle," he said elegantly, bowing his head to her briefly. "I shall contemplate these calories for the rest of the evening." He placed the dish and spoon gently on the table in front of him and struck a sober pose. "There, I'm starting to feel full already," he said.

"Jo-Seppy!" said Rita. "I'm not kidding. You're getting thin! Isn't he Jenny?"

Attention turned to Genevieve, who was doing a wretched job of trying to conceal the subject on her mind.

Joseph answered before Genevieve could gather up a reply. "Can't you see the poor woman is busy sitting on a pin cushion? This is no time to nag her about my dietary shortcomings." Joseph had noticed her reaction to the question about Gerry Kiplinger, and though he had his own opinion of what might lie behind it, he left it to the others to attempt to draw it out.

Genevieve did indeed have a pained and uncomfortable look on her face, but colored immediately as Rita and George turned to look at her.

"Oh! Jenny, what is the matter?" said Rita with a small amount of distress.

"Nothing, nothing at all!" she said with almost convincing normality as she dropped a cherry on the carpet and spilled iced tea in her lap.

Joseph pretended to study a manuscript while the others fussed to clean up the spill. I must truly be getting old, he thought. It all seems so obvious to me, yet hopelessly, impossibly distant. Was I once young enough to be unaware of the transparency of human emotions and turmoil?

Fifteen minutes later Joseph had grown impatient. Neither Rita nor George had gotten Genevieve to say what was on her mind, nor even expressed sufficient curiosity as far as he was concerned. He couldn't stand it any more. Age has to have some privilege, he thought, and I hereby exercise it.

"I've been hearing rumors," said Joseph, "that George is considered very marriageable here in Silverdale. Isn't that right, Jenny?"

Joseph expected her to blush again or become flustered, making it more obvious to the other two that she was very much in love with George, but he was startled when Genevieve spoke right up with perfect composure.

"Oh my! Has she been talking to you, too? Here I was thinking it was a secret she had with me. Come to think of it, though, she isn't the type to keep a secret, now is she?"

"Wait a minute, wait a minute," said Rita while her father industriously ignored the conversation. "Who are you talking about?"

Joseph remained silent, privately scolding himself for having been off the mark.

"Gerry Kiplinger," said Genevieve. "She told me flat out she was expecting George to propose to her." She glanced sideways to see how George was taking it, only to turn back with a jolt when he burst out laughing.

"Now that's funny!" said George. Rita joined the laughter upon seeing her father's unusually droll reaction, and Joseph raised his eyebrows humorously.

"But she's practically an old lady," objected Rita, "and she doesn't even know Daddy. She just likes to boss him around—"

"I wish I could tell you she was joking," said Genevieve, "but she was serious. I'm sure of it. Might you have encouraged her in some way without intending it?" she asked George delicately.

George scratched his head, considering. "Well, I don't think I ever insulted her."

"You never insult anybody, Daddy," said Rita.

"I said thank you to her every time she helped with Rita's performances," George said.

"In other words," said Joseph, "the woman has fabricated this rumor out of thin air."

"Jo-Seppy, you're too blunt" cried Rita.

"They're just pulling my leg, Rita," said George.

"Oh no," said Genevieve. "It's really true, George. Gerry said she thought you would be announcing the engagement at the tea, and she asked me what I thought she should wear to the wedding."

George looked extremely puzzled. "You may not think of it much," continued Genevieve to George, "but you and Rita are famous in Silverdale. I think there may be several more ladies who have the same hopes as Gerry, but she is a little more outspoken—"

"Blunderingly obvious, she means," interjected Joseph, and Rita ran over and sat on the arm of his chair so she could clamp a hand over his mouth.

"—than the rest. Really, I don't think most of them see half of the real opportunity; to marry a man of such kindness and character, who would care for a wife just as well as he cares for his daughter, who loves all the best things in life and has not a single vice, who is the soul of humility without even trying, who is everything a good Christian woman could honor and obey—"

"It's true, Daddy!" said Rita, and Joseph returned the favor of clamping a hand over her mouth. George's face had assumed an expression that seemed to say, "Are you talking about me?"

"—but who obviously does not wish to remarry—" continued Genevieve until George interrupted her.

"I never said that," he cut in very swiftly.

"Oh—well, of course people assumed that, that you were not interested, because you never.... you never..." She trailed off, losing her short-lived eloquence and coloring deeply.

"Now that we've established Gerry Kiplinger does seek the hand of George in matrimony," said Joseph, "and that she seeks it for reasons perhaps slightly unjustified—there, Rita; that wasn't so blunt, was it?—and that George is not totally opposed to remarrying, it might be wise to take action of some sort. We must assume that if George does not propose to Gerry, she will propose to him. Soon. So what do you say George?"

"No." He said it so abruptly and with such a faint hint of distaste that everyone laughed.

"If you did happen to have someone else in mind," said Joseph, "perhaps you could put off any unwanted offers by declaring where your true affections lie."

A long silence ensued while George considered this, looking at Rita, then inward, back to Rita again, and so forth. "Right," he said at last. The others waited in silence and suspense as he rose and stood in his place, pausing lengthily.

George turned toward Genevieve, kneeled and took her hand, then said, "Will you marry me, Jenny?"

Genevieve turned white with shock and started to lose consciousness, but George grasped her arms and was saying, "You don't have to. I'm sorry. It's all right."

Color began to return to Genevieve's cheeks just as Rita rushed over, so she stopped and slipped slowly back to Joseph's chair.

"Are you sure?" asked Genevieve feebly. "I'm so plain compared to some of those other ladies who could help you with Rita's career. I—" She seemed to collect herself and smiled. "But of course you didn't mean it—it was just a joke, wasn't it?"

George's eyes were floorward as he obviously groped for words. He sighed and made a few gestures as if he were going to begin speaking, but no words came.

Genevieve's eyes widened slightly as he finally looked in her eyes. What passed between them in that moment served her for an answer, because she said "Oh my!" with twelve variations as layers of disbelief peeled away and new thoughts occurred to her.

George must have been encouraged, because he gently repeated his question. "Will you?"

Genevieve smiled. "What a thought!" she whispered. "This is the happiest thing that has happened to me in years and years! I just didn't expect it."

George took this to mean yes, and said, " I've been thinking all these years what a kind person you are, and how much you help others, and it's been a wish of mine to give back to you at least as much as you've given—"

Joseph led Rita quietly out of the room and through the French doors to the back yard. The sun was low on the horizon and the air was still very warm.

"How do you like this new match, my little student?" said Joseph.

"I think I'm almost as shocked as Jenny!" Rita exclaimed. "I never thought of either one of them as the type to get romantically involved, I guess you would say. But they do know each other well, they get along perfectly, I love them both to pieces, and—"

"Will you like a stepmother?" he asked.

She looked at him abruptly. "I don't know," she said distractedly, thinking of the past. "I didn't know my mother well, you know. And, poor thing, I don't think she had a very good time being a mother because of her illnesses. Do you remember when we first met, and you told me that you don't live your life the way it is in the books?"

"I do," he replied.

"Well, I've remembered that all these years. I used to compare my life to books—back then, I mean—and it was always backwards. Instead of having a wicked stepmother, I had a real mother, who was—you know. I thought I worked so hard to be a good girl, but somehow I was always in trouble. No magic happened in my life, except maybe a little bit at school when the teacher was nice to me. But then I met you. I had a feeling about it when I first saw that piano. And then when you told me you didn't live your life the way it was in the books, I thought, "Here is someone like me!"

"And then you learned that I was, after all, just a grumpy old man."

"No I didn't!"

"All right. Perhaps we have something in common. But my opinion of your father's match, even though you didn't ask for it, and I have no right to waggle my jaws at this hour, is that we could not wish for a better match, or better timing for it."

"Oh, I agree!" she said. "It just took me by surprise. The more I think of it, though, the more it seems just right. I'd so much rather have Jenny for a stepmother than anyone else I can think of in Silverdale."

The engagement of George and Jenny was announced at Rita's tea, but not without carefully circulating the rumor beforehand so that Gerry would be prepared. It perturbed her intensely at first, but she was so determined to make a success of the tea at her house that she had no choice but to take it gracefully in public.

Rita's University Recital went beautifully and she received a small but favorable review in the newspaper as well as the admiration of all the members of the School of Music who attended. Joseph introduced her to several of the Professors at the tea afterwards, and when they had finally returned home and gotten a good night's sleep, he was curious to know her impression of each.

"They were all very great and distinguished," she said, "but so different from you, Jo-Seppy."

"Younger by twenty or thirty years, I dare say," he answered.

"Not just that. I'm glad you're my teacher."

"But when you go to University to study, one of them will be your teacher. Do you have any preferences?"

"What?" cried Rita. "I want you to be my teacher! I don't want another teacher. What are you talking about?"

"You must move on some time, Rita. You will outgrow me. I have my limits, in ability as well as in life span."

"Jo-Seppy, you are not allowed to talk like that!" she snapped. "You're going to live to be a hundred; probably two hundred. And no one could ask for a better teacher."

Joseph decided he might as well open the discussion on this topic now. While he didn't want to alarm her about what he had learned at the doctor's office that day, she must confront the fact that he was 67 years old and entering the final phase of his life. Her optimism could be directed beneficially toward her own future and career, but to waste it on hoping for an extension of his life would be wrong.

"Anyone my age is allowed a great deal of leeway, in cultured circles, Mademoiselle. So let me have my say and then we will leave this subject, I promise."

"I don't like this subject, but for your sake I will let you have your say," she said.

He closed the piano but stayed at the bench, quiet for a moment.

"Let me keep it brief," he continued. "As we know, these mortal husks will not last forever, and I really have only one important wish to be carried out after I am gone. One wish that I request of you."

Rita looked at him intently, her smile fading rapidly and skin looking slightly paler, waiting.

"Every moment we have spent together preparing you for your future has been of great enjoyment to me. Just in case there is, as some say, a Heaven—well, maybe I wouldn't end up there!—but perhaps an Afterlife, I want you to carry on with your life and career in a way that would make me glad to have been your teacher. Consider that I will be watching over your shoulder, because I will if it is in any way possible. Do you promise?"

Rita looked deeply into his eyes and he watched her eyes grow shiny with tears until one was spilling onto her cheek. She buried her face in his shoulder and did not let go for some minutes.

What an idiot I am, he thought. Now she knows.

"I promise," she finally said. Then she excused herself and ran off. When she returned a few minutes later, she was in control of herself.

"I let you have your say, and now I'm going to have mine!" she announced. "I am going to take you with me to the University. I'll have some other teachers too, if you insist, but you have to give me lessons too," she said.

"I suppose we could work something out."

"And you are going to hear all my recitals, because how will you know how I'm doing otherwise? It would be bad luck for me if you weren't there. And don't worry about driving because I'm sure Daddy and Jenny will take you with them. Oh, did I tell you they're getting married on October 15?"

"Why, no—"

"That gives them three months to plan, and Jenny insisted on that much time but Daddy wanted the wedding to be as soon as possible. Did you know he's been saving money for a new house for four years and no one even knew it? Not me, or Jenny, or anyone!"

"I didn't know—"

"But they're just going to have a short honeymoon for now because I will be in school and too much will be happening, and they have to decide where to buy a house, but there will be plenty of time to work that out in the next year or so. Aren't you excited about the wedding?"

"Yes, I am rather—"

"I'm going to be the Maid of Honor!"

"I hope you can stop talking long enough for them to say 'I do.' There! I finally got a whole sentence in edgewise," said Joseph.

"Jo-Seppy!" cried Rita, playfully scowling.

"I think I have a right to complain," said Joseph.

"You have no right to complain!" she said. "You got one promise out of me, and now I'm going to get one out of you. You have to promise me. Promise me that you will be there when I sing my first opera. You have to be there. Do you promise?"

"All right," he declared. "I promise. Though snow, sleet, hail, or my own absentmindedness may threaten to interfere, I will persevere until I am seated in the front row on your opening night. I have spoken, and nothing can stop me," he said, and pounded an imaginary gavel on an imaginary podium.

Rita bowed and then leapt onto the bench next to him and showed him the arias she wanted to prepare for her next recital.

Joseph had a successful surgery in September, and was surprised that he was alive and well to see Rita begin her University education two years later. Joseph sold his old Silverdale house when the Henleys sold theirs to move to the city, near the University that Rita would attend. He rented a small bedroom in the new Henley house, while his piano resided in the living room. Genevieve and George had a ten-month-old son and the household seemed to run smoothly with Genevieve's care, George's industriousness and the artistic endeavors of Joseph and Rita.

When she had sung operettas in high school and excerpts from an opera in college, Rita had made it very clear that she did not consider any of these her "first opera."

"Listen to me, Jo-Seppy," she said the week before the first of these. "This is not an opera, okay? You promised to hear my first opera."

"Mademoiselle, you think that I would be confused about what an opera is or is not?" he said, pretending to be insulted.

"Of course not," she said. "But I just want you to know you won't get away with anything."

"Very well, Mademoiselle," he replied. "I can't blame you for turning the tables on me after I have made you sing your vocal exercises as perfectly as you have."

Rita excelled and by the age of 22 had completed her degree and successfully auditioned to join the opera company. She sang in the chorus initially, but had her first major role when she was 25. Her two little half-brothers Benjamin and Joshua, six and eight years old, sat in front row seats with Joseph, George and Genevieve for this milestone in her life.

Neither Rita or Joseph spoke of the fact that Joseph's promise had been kept. He was 76 now and hoped for nothing more in life now that he had seen Rita succeed. Enough aches, pains and inconveniences accompanied old age that he would have been glad to call it a life. He had more than himself to consider, however. He had a place in the family and his responsibilities included everything from being Rita's advisor and confidante to baby-sitting little Joshua on occasion. His wry remarks could be counted upon, and his piano and cabinets full of music as well as his scholarly approach to life and music lent a cultivated atmosphere to the otherwise simple and happy home of the Henleys.

Five years passed, with Rita spending less and less time at home as she was booked for tours around the U.S. and Europe. Joseph had accompanied her on several of the early tours but now was feeling far too slow to keep up with them. He felt strangely content staying at home and idly watching the goings on. The Henley boys were on the edge of teenagerhood and it fascinated Joseph to listen to their talk. He found it amazingly like that of his own boyhood in spirit even though different in actual words.

One evening it became very clear to him that he needed to see Rita. He told George, and could see by George's expression that his request was taken seriously. Even though she was in the middle of a European tour, Rita arrived the next evening.

"Jo-Seppy, how good to see you, and much sooner than I thought!" she cried when she rushed in the door, as Joseph sat alone in the living room at his piano. The Henleys had picked her up at the airport and then discreetly gone on a brief family outing after leaving off Rita at home.

"Music to my ears," he said from the piano bench, lacking the energy to turn around to see her and not caring because he could picture her perfectly. "It's been too long since I've heard you sing in La Traviata."

"Yes, I know," she sighed. "My life is a mess right now. I don't know whether I'm coming or going. I think back on the struggle of those early opera days as pleasant memories now. But how are you?" She had taken off her coat and came over to sit on the edge of his bench and grasp his hands. He still did not look at her.

"I am appalled at how old this body has gotten while I've been busy attending to other things," he said. "I don't even remember where my business cards are now so that I can show people what my name is when I forget it. Do you suppose I have that old-person disease? I forget the name of it just now, of course, but that's to be expected."

"You don't fool me, Jo-seppy! I heard you playing the Habanera when I came up to the doorstep. I remember dancing up and down your old hallway as a little girl with a rose between my teeth when you would play that for me, in the old, old days. You have a better memory than anyone I know. For the important things."

"Thank you, Mademoiselle," he said, finally looking at her and smiling gently. "Which brings me to one of the important things I was trying to remember to ask you about."

"Oh it does?" she said as she rose. "You will have to wait for just a bit while I get something to eat or I won't be able to answer. I couldn't eat a thing on the plane because it was so horribly unappealing. All I could think of was getting home and having our favorite snack together."

"Swiss cheese?" he inquired.

She laughed. "That proves it! You are not only your usual ironic self, but you remember perfectly the one food that I absolutely hate."

"Yes, but that's no consolation for being utterly at a loss to remember what you might be referring to as our favorite snack. In fact, I'm sure I've forgotten everything I've ever eaten. Is one supposed to pay attention to such things?"

"Only if one wants to," she answered as she walked to the kitchen. "I knew that subject would get you going!" She popped briefly back into the living room from the kitchen to add, "It was my favorite snack I was referring to, but I always think of you and of home when I eat it. Remember—I would eat honey blintzes with Viennese coffee on lazy Sunday afternoons, while you played opera themes for the family and told us all about their history?"

"Ah, yes," he admitted. "I remember you eating those rolled up little things, but I didn't know their fancy name. I remember more clearly the aroma of that coffee. It was pleasant."

"That's what I thought! So I'm making up some of that for us. Jenny said she made some blintzes and left them in the refrigerator for us, so I'll heat those up, too, if you'll just give me a few minutes!"

He sighed, and played a Bach pastorale. When she returned with the coffee and blintzes, he got up slowly from the bench and joined her on the couch. She came over to assist when she saw the difficulty he was having.

"Old age is inconvenience in spades."

"Perhaps a medical genius will cure it some day," Rita said from the kitchen. "Maybe not in time for you and me, but one of these days. They've all but cured infant mortality, they can even cure cancer some of the time, and many of the childhood diseases and plagues. Why not old age?"

"Because old age is the supreme plague. Everyone dies of it if they don't die of something else first," he grumbled.

"Do you think the human race will evolve a super-genius who can outwit death?" Rita asked.

"I can tell you that if he outwitted old age he would be most of the way there," said Joseph. "It's enough to make anyone lie down and die."

"I disagree," said Rita. "Too many people are quite content to die of something other than old age. Remember the martyrs and soldiers, just to mention a couple of types."

"Oh, a pox upon those types. I've never understood them. But let me point out that the martyrs, and perhaps many of the soldiers, believed that death was not the end; that it only released them to a better existence. Heaven, Valhalla, what have you. Who, these days, runs around with the kind of certainty those fellows had? They are mostly a thing of the past. We live in a world of disposable dishes, packages, appliances, cars, people. And a disposable Joseph Steinman...." he muttered mostly to himself, though Rita heard him. She was finishing a bite of blintz and took a sip of coffee before replying.

"Jo-Seppy, if I didn't know what a tease you are, I'd be worried."

"Crank might be a better term for me than tease. And now that you've got the confounded snacks, may I proceed?"

"Yes, yes; but you must let me say something first."

"Age before beauty is the custom I believe—"

"It's short," Rita interrupted. "It may make your question to me unnecessary. I want you to know—I regret how selfish I have been in the past, and I feel I had no right to attempt to dictate where or how or how long you live your life. I—whether God or some other force I do not understand determines the length and breadth of a person's life, I know it is certainly not in my hands. I am sorry—it must appear to you that I am callous to your suffering, wishing only to keep you here for my own benefit."

She looked up at that point and he had such a look of surprise on his face that she stopped.

"What is it?" she asked.

"That is the last thing I expected you to say. And it makes me feel rather silly about what I'm going to say, but one must nevertheless be honest, don't you think?" He didn't let her reply, but continued.

"But let me say first that there is no need at all for you to apologize to me. You have never seemed callous, you have never made me feel that you were selfish. I think we have both done and been whatever we have been to each other willingly and happily. If I complain too much of old age, count it as one of my many flaws. But don't take it seriously."

"Jo-Seppy—"

"Now, before I doze off, let me finish. My question is, have you considered getting married?"

She laughed a little. "What put that notion into your head? Don't tell me you called me away from the tour to ask me that? I've told you all my ridiculous tales of suitors from the absurd to the pathetic, and I thought we had laughed that subject away into impossibility. There isn't anyone out there who is right for me. At least not among the ones who think they want a professional musician for a wife."

"Well, it is worth some thought," he answered. "I've been thinking in these last few weeks; you know, when they think I'm dozing in the chair I'm actually having wild flights of contemplation. I've been thinking of Joseph

Steinman, the human being. He got a few things done with his life, after all, but there is one thing he did not do. He did not replace himself. I produced no offspring. I don't necessarily regret that or think I have missed fatherhood as a calling, but it did occur to me that if very many people neglected that duty, then activities would get a trifle scarce here on earth. Reproduction of life is part of the overall plan, as it seems to exist now. So, I wanted to undo any bias I may have put into your thinking on that subject. You have absorbed so much of my knowledge and love of music that I wonder if perhaps there was any contamination. You know what an eccentric old fool I can be."

"Well, not eccentric necessarily," Rita said, "but maybe just plain outlandish! You have not contaminated me! What an idea! As long as we're on the subject of marriage, however, I will admit that I have thought of it from time to time, just lately. I have seen how nice it is for Daddy and Jenny. They have the boys, but you and I—we are sort of oddballs. Sometimes I think it would be nice to have a slow and simple life, at least for a while."

"It is nice," said Joseph. "I've been living the slow and simple life and I recommend it, at least for certain persons for periods of time. It's done me good. But then, I am on a different time table than you."

Rita looked at him. "Maybe I could have enough children to replace both of us, if I get busy," she said.

Joseph smiled. "Always eager to please. You go right ahead and have as many or as few children as you like. But I have one more thing to confess."

His face was suddenly so drawn that Rita was alarmed. She went to his side and gripped his hands, looking into his eyes.

"I'm not having a heart attack, Mademoiselle; just an unpleasant memory. Don't worry."

"All right. Are you sure you want to talk about it?" she asked.

"Yes. It's haunted me for years. I finally understand why. I somehow felt responsible for Marie's death, which was absurd because it was an illness and a terrible misfortune that no one diagnosed and treated her in time. So why did I feel so bad? Of course it was hard to lose her, hard to lose my hopes for her future, hard to see youth and beauty fail so soon, but—I did not see until this week why I could not get it out of my mind. I remember that she and I had a disagreement in the last few months before her death. I don't mean that we ever argued or had any bitter words. It was just that she once spoke wishfully of having a husband and children, as if it might be in her near future. I lectured her immediately on her duty as a performer and artist, and that to achieve the goal that was hers to reach she would need to devote herself to it completely and without reservation, not diluting it with other lesser goals.

"I will never forget the look on her face. I saw that I was coming across too harshly to her, and tried to soften it, but the more I spoke the more her eyes filled with water, and she finally turned and would not look at me. She left without speaking and things were not the same again after. I didn't understand what I had done wrong. I had said what I believed was correct, what would lead to her success. For some reason now I can look back and understand what she felt—how odd. It is quite painful; a physical pain right here," and he indicated his chest.

"I wish I could ask her forgiveness. I am fairly sure that what I told her was wrong. At least it was the wrong thing to say to her. She took my word to be truth, which I often foolishly believed it was. How I wish I could ask her forgiveness."

Joseph was beginning to pale, so Rita helped him to lie down and make himself comfortable. "I'm sure she forgives you, Jo-Seppy. Don't worry. Things do come out all right in the end. Just as you understand her now, I'm sure she understands why you said what you did, wherever she is. Please don't worry about that. Just relax and get some rest. You need some rest."

"Yes, I'm so tired. Thank you, my dear."

He drifted off and Rita spent an hour watching him as the blintzes grew cold, until the rest of the family came home. George checked his pulse and then covered him lightly and let him sleep on the couch for the night.

Sometime in the middle of the night, Joseph felt a glorious, spacious feeling. He felt better than he had in years. It was dark, but he thought he would just get up and stretch. He wondered why he could see everything so clearly in the dark. In fact, he was extremely curious about how it was that he could see his own body lying on the couch, sleeping. He assumed he was dreaming and enjoyed the floating feeling until the dawn came.

Eventually the family woke and tried to wake him, but he would not awake. From all the flurry that ensued, he deduced that he was dreaming of his own death. He felt detached enough from it that it didn't bother him a bit. This is ludicrously melodramatic, he thought. What are they crying about? I feel fine. I'm right here.

It was not until his body had been carried out of the house to the funeral parlor that he began to understand he was not dreaming. He was alone in the house. There was no body. Just himself; as a soul? He presumed so. So this is it, he thought. Heavens, now what am I supposed to do?

Joseph said good-bye to the house and to its inhabitants, in absentia, and willed himself upward, wondering what awaited him.

A Flash of Life

By Amit Kapoor

Dark skies.
Two lonely spots
of cloud—moving
towards each other,
Pushed, by strong
gales of passion;
They strike,
They rub
against each other,
causing friction;
Producing
A flash of Divine Light,
Producing
the Life Force—
Present one moment—
Gone the next.

FLEET CATS IN ACTION

By Slate Bender

Deviled Plagues

By Colette Bree, 1999

Perry wiped the sweat from his brow. He had been toiling in the heat of the day for ten hours, assisting the doctor in seeing first the sick children, then the sick mothers, and finally any others in the village who needed medical attention. At last the sun was sinking and the line of people ended.

He'd forgotten to eat that day, except for the coffee and bread for breakfast and two bites of a sandwich that were interrupted when the mother of a feverish boy came to plead for his attention. Perry shuffled over to his tent and collapsed on the cot. He was feeling a bit feverish himself, so he took some antibiotics and decided he would take a short nap before trying to find some dinner.

This wasn't how he had expected it to be. He had wanted to share the Word of God with these neglected people, but it was hard to get them to listen when they were diseased, hungry and tormented with pain. He was able to procure medical supplies and food with donations from his home city in America, but getting actual medical personnel out here was difficult. He often caught himself starting to have the thought that Mr. Average American Citizen only cared about lining his own pocket—and maybe the pockets of his children—but he would ward off such critical thoughts by reciting First Corinthians 13 to himself. He needed to love all people without judgment. He must not think ill of anyone. He appreciated the thousands of dollars donated for medical supplies and for his sustenance, but it would have been nice to have some actual, physical *help* in what he was doing.

Perry had no medical license or formal training, but when the occasional doctor came out for a summer or a year he had learned the basics of how to stitch and dress wounds, how to administer antibiotics and vaccinations, how to treat dysentery and parasite infestations. He performed miracles as far as the people were concerned. He went from village to village, doing what he could to take care of their requests for help and always despairing because there was little time to enlighten them about the Gospel.

That evening as Perry fried himself some corn meal mush for dinner, he got to wondering about things. After he ate and cleaned up, he knelt by his cot and prayed in earnest.

"Dear God," he began, "thank you for the blessings of the day, thank you for allowing me to help the people, thank you for giving me enough to eat. I have a question, though. I have served you many years. I am out here alone with few books to study, no wise scholars to consult. There is something I don't understand. I am trying so hard to bring your word to these people, but how can I hope to reach them all? I don't understand why these poor people must go to hell just because they didn't hear and understand your word before disease or war takes them. For that matter, I'm having trouble understanding why there should be a hell at all. I can't understand how the God of infinite love can allow the devil to have any of his loved ones.

Perry sighed. "I know I am probably not worthy of knowing the answer, and I accept my punishment in advance for the question, but I had to say in prayer what you know very well has been in my heart. Forgive me. Amen."

He crossed himself and stood to make his final preparations for bed, only to cry out in amazement to discover someone standing in front of him.

"Yo," the person said.

"I beg your pardon?" said Perry.

"You had a question, right dude?" said the person. "God said you had a question, and I'm here to give you the answer, straight from the horse's mouth."

"I don't understand," said Perry. The person speaking to him was tall and wiry, perhaps eighteen years old in appearance, and was wearing very baggy pants that sagged a couple of inches below his drab boxer shorts. His hair was literally standing on end in spikes and he wore rings in each ear and in his nose.

"Come on, bro! Was it or was it not you that was just praying to God here with a question about hell?"

"Well, yes, that was me, but—"

"So here I am. The devil himself. If you can't believe me, who can you believe?" He smiled confidently.

Perry's legs gave way and he fell onto his cot. "You don't look like—why do you look like *that*?"

"Oh this," said the devil, looking at his outfit. "Special project."

"Who are you really," said Perry, "and how did you get here? Do you need help?"

"If you want to know who I am *really*," said the devil, "let me start at the beginning. He pulled up a straw chair and sat down. "Would you like a coke?"

"No, thank you," said Perry as the devil withdrew a 12 ounce can of Coke out of his pocket and opened it. He took a big swig of it.

"I was an angel once, but I got in trouble. I guess that story's been passed on, hasn't it?"

Perry nodded, wondering if his fever was causing him to hallucinate. He felt his forehead, but it was quite a normal temperature.

"Makes me look like a really bad guy," continued the devil, "but actually I was once one of God's favorites. Everyone forgets about all the good things I did and just thinks of my fall. That's why I've been trying my darnedest to get back in God's good graces. As my punishment, God assigned me the task of setting all these Earth people straight. Man, I just about lost it when He told me that."

Perry blinked rapidly in disbelief.

"I couldn't believe it either, dude. I thought that was a pretty stiff punishment, as it could go on for millions of years, you know, judging by what I had to work with. But I didn't really have a choice, did I? So, I set about trying to get these people to behave themselves.

"I used to use real serious, on-the-spot punishments—lightning bolts and stuff like that—but it didn't really work. I got quite a few of the worst ones killed off, but then instead of scaring the rest of them into behaving, it just inspired them to think of ways to avoid lightning. Then all these cults sprang up about offering sacrifices. Bribes, dude. I was getting nowhere.

"One of the things I tried after that was to get the word spread around that people who didn't behave were going to go to hell, where they would burn not just to death, but *forever*. Thought for sure that'd do the trick. But do you know what those rascals did? They got this big racket going with high church officials accepting money and bribes and living high off the hog, promising the rest of the people they would go to heaven instead of hell if they just contributed enough to the religious coffers. And if it wasn't that then it was wars over religious differences or tortures to purify people.

"About that time I just took a vacation for a while. I mean, after six thousand years of effort on this ball of dirt I was pretty discouraged. I did throw a few hints into the dreams of some of the more intelligent men before I went to the Big Dipper Resort, and by the time I got back there was a Renaissance brewing. I started changing my mind about Purgatory."

"I've wondered about that," said Perry, forgetting how implausible was the fact that he was talking to the devil.

"Yeah, man, it's this idea that you go in some kind of holding tank after you kick the bucket. In actual fact, some of these souls were so beat up after their lives here they didn't have the will to start over again, like the rules state. You know it's just not legal on this planet to be walking around without a biological form, and people kind of politely ignore the ones who are gauche enough to do that. Anyway, I was kind of letting the folks stack up in there—in Purgatory, I mean—until I could figure out what to do next, but I started running out of space.

"That's when I got my brilliant idea. Fresh from my vacation, I was really inspired to get on with my project here and try to wrap it up in less than a thousand years. I figured I would force these dudes in Purgatory, or wherever they were hiding, to come on out and take another form. I thought I could whip up some really clever instructive situations for them. Sort of teach them a lesson, you know.

"I had great fun with that for a while, until I noticed my low success rate. For example, I had this one dude who scared a lot of pretty young girls by being a voyeur, so I had him come back as a toilet seat. Unusual, yes, but I thought that after seeing enough undersides of people he would have his fill of it and get off that kick. Not to mention the limitations of being able to do nothing but sit there and be sat on! This dude, however, liked it! He's happy as a clam to this day, being a public toilet seat. Oh man, did I goof that one up!

"A few times I tried sending plagues to a large group of people so they'd have to get smart and take care of each other instead of fighting. Or die off. You'd be surprised how often they chose to die off. I'd have bossy mother-in-laws come back as hen-pecked husbands with even grouchier mother-in-laws. I'd have murderers come back as cockroaches a few hundred times until they got really familiar with the feeling of being stepped on. I'd have thieves come back as retarded children and robber barons as children of poverty-stricken, single, ex-prostitute, drug addict mothers. Sometimes I even worked on a grander scale with whole bunches of people--like the time I took some of the more notoriously cruel slaveholders and put a bug in their ear to join the Jimmy Jones religion a couple lives down the road.

"The bottom line was that it just didn't work, though," said the devil. He finished the last of his coke. "Can you guess why?"

"No, I can't," admitted Perry.

"Either can I," said the devil.

"Have you considered trying love and mercy?" asked Perry timidly.

"That was the first thing I tried. That's how God operates, after all. But I just wasn't getting through to the people here. I spent hundreds of years going around being nice to everybody, ignoring their bad deeds and telling them personally to just behave and treat each other well, follow the rules, get along, and so forth, and it just didn't seem to help matters. Many of them tried but couldn't do it. I mean, this was a real problem, dude. If it was just a matter of love and mercy, we would have been done millenniums ago!"

"I see," said Perry. "Um, would you mind terribly answering another question? I mean, as long as you're here."

"Shoot," said the devil.

"You said something about plagues a bit ago. Do you have anything to do with these people I've been—you know, the people here and all their illnesses?"

"Cut me a break!" said the devil. "I'm not that stupid. It didn't work after several tries, so I gave it up. But the horrible thing is that it's been copied all over the planet. I don't know how they do it, but people manage now to come up with all kinds of diseases and illnesses and plagues all the time. It's like a bad thing seems to spread like wildfire in this place, but anything good and sensible gets a bunch of flack and resistance."

"Oh my," said Perry. "I didn't mean to accuse you of anything ... I was just curious."

"No problem, bro," said the devil. "Any more questions before I go?"

"Well," said Perry, "do I understand you correctly to say that hell was just something you made up to scare people? That there is no such thing, really?"

"Yes and no," said the devil. He looked at Perry carefully. "I'm going to tell you the truth, but I don't want you to let it get to you. The fact is that you are already in hell, for all intents and purposes. This is pretty much it, bro. It doesn't get any worse than this. Sorry."

"What?" said Perry in disbelief. His mouth hung open. "How could God put me in hell? How could a loving and merciful God do that when I have served Him all my life?"

"Hey dude, I didn't say God put you here. I'm just saying it's got some major problems and this is where you are right now. Cheer up, though. There *is* an escape ladder."

"Where??" said Perry. "Where, where?"

"You wouldn't believe me if I told you right now. But keep up the good work. I wish they were all as far along as you. Later, bro."

The devil put on his Walkman, turned up the volume, danced out of the tent and disappeared into the night.

The World Is...

By Amit Kapoor

The World
Is but a tap—a closed tap—
Not turned off tightly.

Ever heard
The wailings within the tap?
Not having the pressure
To gush forth freely
In streams of emotions,
It lets out
The still sad music
Of humanity—
Sometimes squeaking,
Sometimes screaming—
Without the power
To quench the thirst,
Without the ability
To flow as fountains—
Just crying,
Trying to make us let her free.

Open the tap
And unchoke the world;
Unstrangulate it—
And let her live on.

A Source of Lightness

By Kendall Roman, 2001

Emilio walked into the desert town with a great thirst. He walked into the first establishment that offered a promise of anything liquid, which happened to be a tavern.

"I'll have a soda water, please," he said to the bartender.

The bartender shoved it at him. There were maybe eight other men in the tavern who watched him with mild interest and strong suspicion.

Emilio sat down and tried to drink his soda as slowly as possible. The other men gradually relaxed and began to get back to their gossip. As he had his back to them, he didn't know who was saying what.

"Did you hear that Senor Gordon is on his deathbed?"

"No!"

"Yes. And the end will be soon."

"I guess we'll have a new widow in town."

"Whoooo!" accompanied by various hoots and hollers.

"No doubt she will be worth a pretty penny."

"But what would you do with her after you got married and got the money is what I want to know. She's as cold as ice."

"She makes my skin crawl."

"She wouldn't marry you anyway!"

"She'd marry me before she'd marry you!"

Gutteral laughter.

"Once she looked at me like her eyes were going to burn a hole through my head. Just because I was ripping off some young kid. Everybody does it. She's naive."

"I think she's read too many books and she doesn't know what life is like for real people."

"Not bad looking, though."

"Well, that depends on which part you're talking about, doesn't it?" More laughter and snorting.

"I bet you a hundred pesos you wouldn't have the courage to go courting her."

"Nice, Juan. You've never had a hundred pesos at one time in your life."

"I have so. I bet you a hundred pesos, Rodrigo."

"Save your money. She thinks she's too good for you. I can tell already. She thinks she's too good for everybody."

"What difference does that make? Any woman's mind can be changed with enough beating. Why would she be any different?"

"Jorge, you do *too* much beating. Everybody knows that. You don't see none of *us* getting thrown in jail for it, do you?"

"No, but at least I got a well-behaved wife."

"If you don't count the times she runs away every other week."

There were sounds of imminent fighting, but the bartender hurried over with more beer and they were distracted for the moment.

Emilio turned around after he ordered his second soda and addressed the group of men. "Who is this fine senora you have been honoring with your speeches?"

After the raucous laughter died down, one of the men said, "No one who would interest you."

"On the contrary," said Emilio, "I am very interested. Why would any civilized man not be interested in a woman of beauty, dignity and reserve? These are the classic virtues in a female."

A few grunted. "The only virtue that woman has is her money. Senor Gordon is filthy rich," said Rodrigo.

"Filthy rich is perhaps true, but not necessarily a virtue," said Emilio.

"That's what you think!" said Jorge. "It's a virtue to me."

"Yes, well, are you gentleman cooking up a plan then to woo the widow and split the money between you?" asked Emilio. "Surely with all your gentlemanly charms combined, all your wit, all your ideas, you could win her fortune."

A few seconds of silence allowed the idea to soak in, and then a new round of derision and taunting began. Emilio slipped out in the middle of this, as he was the doctor who had been called to Senor Gordon's death bed, and he was now just as curious to meet Senora Gordon as he was to meet the Senor.

"Thank you for coming, Dr. Vasquez," said Senora Gordon. "The local doctor could do nothing for him. Please be honest with me after your examination, but speak with me before you upset your patient with any bad news. Please."

"Yes, of course, Senora," said Emilio. "Give me fifteen minutes alone with him and I will tell you what I can."

Emilio had suspected that the men in the tavern were cowed by Senora Gordon's beauty and grace, and therefore compelled to criticize her. She was indeed everything he had expected, and more. She must have been twenty years younger than her husband, who was purported to be barely into his sixties. She had haunting eyes—he could barely look away from them, so deep with suffering and knowing were they. She moved quietly and smoothly, and dressed in light pastel colors. Her hair and skin were fair, a welcome contrast to all the dark skin and hair he had admired in his everyday travels. He wondered about her nationality, but she did speak perfect English. He was very curious to hear how she came to be Senora Gordon, and so hoped for an opportunity to find out.

Senor Gordon, on the other hand, was a frightful sight. First glance indicated that the tavern rumors might be correct. Senor was pale enough and blue enough to indicate impending failure of the circulatory and/or respiratory systems. He was not able to respond to questions verbally, though he could move his head almost imperceptibly in what seemed like attempts to answer questions. After five minutes' examination, Dr. Emilio Vasquez had to agree with the local doctor's diagnosis and treatment. Senor's body was riddled with cancer according to the medical records and he was in tremendous pain, all major organs on the verge of failure. He left the man in peace after giving him an injection.

"Your doctor is right, Senora," Emilio told her. "The end could come any time now. The sooner he is out of his pain, the better."

"He didn't say anything to you, did he?" she asked with some anxiety.

"No, speech seemed to be beyond him," answered Emilio.

"But did he seem to want to say something?" she asked more delicately, almost tremuloulsly.

Emilio looked at her carefully. "I didn't notice that he did. It was all he could do to hear a few of my questions. I noticed he tried to nod his head at times."

"I will confide in you, Dr. Vasquez. Before this illness suddenly broke upon him, I persuaded him to make a change to his will, and it has been my greatest fear that he would try to change it back as he noticed death's approach. While I didn't want him to do that, I also didn't want to deny him the right to fulfillment of his final wishes."

"I understand," said Emilio, wondering what changes she might have asked the man to make.

"Dr. Vasquez," the Senora continued, "I would like you to stay in one of the rooms here until he is gone. That would be a great help to me. I will pay your fees, whatever they are."

"I can do that, Senora."

"Thank you," said Senora Vasqeuz, looking a little relieved. "The maid will come shortly and show you to your room."

Emilio tried to gather information from the maid, but she was entirely unhelpful. He set down his personal bag and took his doctor's bag with him to go check on his patient again. The maid intersected his course and told him that the evening meal would be served in twenty minutes.

The meal was excellent but shared by only three: Senora Gordon, Dr. Vasquez, and Senor Gordon's niece, Senorita Hernandez. Spirits were subdued and there was little opportunity for anything besides pleasantries. Dr. Vasquez left the table to go directly to the sickroom again, where his patient was not doing any better. Senorita Hernandez entered shortly to relieve the maid of sick watch for the next six hours, and Emilio spoke with her briefly outside the sickroom.

"Is your aunt much afraid of widowhood, do you think?" he asked her.

"I think not, Doctor," was her uninformative reply.

"What makes you think so?" he asked.

"She's a cool woman, and independent," said the Senorita. "It took Uncle ten years to persuade her to marry him. At least that's the way he tells the story. He was obsessed with her and would not give up. If she could live unmarried for twenty-nine years, then she will be all right the rest of her life. Even without Uncle's money she was well enough off. She is an attorney."

"Is she?" said Emilio with surprise.

"Not practicing at present, due to Uncle's health, but she was until a few weeks ago. That's how he met her. She handled a potential lawsuit for him. She's a brilliant woman. But—"

"But what?" Emilio asked when Senorita Hernandez did not finish the sentence.

"I don't know exactly," she said. "I never can seem to get to know her. I don't know if she loves Uncle or not."

"I see," said Emilio. "Does she see other men?"

"Oh no, I'm sure she would never do that."

"I meant no offense—"

"Of course not," said the Senorita. "I'm sure my talk about her must sound strange. But remember that she is a Northerner and not raised in our ways. My uncle liked that about her."

"I can understand that," Emilio said. "I'm only questioning you because I find it odd that I was called in as a specialist in a case that was so clearcut. There is not a thing that medicine can do for him besides make some attempt to relieve the pain. He will be passing shortly."

"I think my Aunt does not want any rumors after his death. The people will expect that he had every kind of care that money could buy."

"Yes, of course," said Emilio, and the two parted.

Within two days the matter was done, and Emilio attended the funeral when invited. He too began to wonder if he had become obsessed with the lovely Senora Gordon. He asked her at the Reception if there was anything further he could do to be of assistance before returning to his home town.

"No, Dr. Vasquez. You've been very helpful, though. Thank you for seeing us through this time."

"Do you need any official medical statements, perhaps, or my notes from this time period?" he asked.

"I don't think so. But I'll call you if something comes up. Thank you again."

Dr. Vasquez noticed that he had been dismissed. But he knew himself, and he knew that he would think forever on an unanswered question and eventually have to come back to ask it if he did not ask now.

"You are welcome, Senora Gordon; and I was hoping that the matter of the will came out in your favor."

She looked puzzled.

"You had mentioned," he prompted, "that you feared Senor Gordon would revoke the change in his will at the last moment."

"Oh, that. No, he did not revoke the change. I'd forgotten I even worried about that. It's certainly not a concern now." She smiled, leaving him more puzzled than ever.

"Very well, then," said the doctor. "Call if you need me. I'm a man of many talents." He bowed and left her.

The next week Emilio might have missed the article in the newspaper, but his maid mentioned it to him.

"Look at these fat, no-good bums getting all that money. What's the world coming to?"

Emilio glanced at the picture she was looking at and recognized one of the characters from the tavern on the way to Senor Gordon's house. The headline read, "Wealthy landowner cuts widow out of will and leaves all to commoners." He stared at the article for thirty seconds, grasping how that aligned with what Senora had told him.

"Mimi, call Senora Gordon and invite her to meet me for lunch today. Her phone number is on my desk. I was there just last week to attend to her dying husband."

"Yes, sir. But sir! That's a three-hour drive."

"I know. Do as I say, please."

"All right," she answered, but she was unable to contact the widow by phone. Emilio had his maid research the problem for an hour, then gave up and called Senorita Hernandez himself. He persuaded her to give him some clue as to the whereabouts of Senora Gordon, even fabricating a medical pretense for it. Senorita Hernandez finally gave him the name of a small village on the edge of the desert and he set off immediately.

"But what about your appointments?" pleaded his secretary.

"Cancel them or reschedule them for one of the other doctors," he said as he raced out the door.

By noon he had checked every inn in the village and not found her yet. There was nothing left to do but stroll past every single dwelling and ask passersby. He sat down in the shade for a moment to compose himself, and to persuade himself to quit worrying about what in the world he was doing. Across the road was a pink, two-story building with a tiled roof. The balcony caught his eye, with marble railing that while subtle seemed to out-class the other buildings in the village.

A guitar-bearing man came by in his wide sombrero and began singing outside the balcony. A woman came out onto the balcony to listen. It was Senora Gordon.

The guitarist set his cup out and sang his heart out, keeping an eye on Senora Gordon. She stared off into the distance, however, evidently transported to a different place and time. Emilio watched her through three songs. The guitarist was trying to disguise his impatience at having received nothing in his cup after three songs. Emilio walked over and filled it to the brim with coins.

"Thank you, Senor!" he said, and continued on his way.

"Good afternoon, Senora Gordon," said Emilio, as she had still not noticed her surroundings.

"Oh! Good afternoon, doctor. I'm afraid I was daydreaming."

"That's quite all right. And please call me Emilio."

"All right, Emilio. I am Francesca."

"Thank you," said Emilio. "May I buy you lunch, Francesca, or a drink?"

"Why don't you come inside? We can have the maid bring some food for you. I'll tell her to show you in. Unless—do you have a house call to make? I'm surprised to see you in this remote village."

"Actually I came here to talk with you after I saw the article in the paper," he admitted.

She smiled. "I haven't paid any attention to the newspapers, but I can imagine they're having a field day."

"You are correct," he said.

They lunched together, and Emilio asked her about the will. "Do I understand correctly that you persuaded your husband to cut you *out* of his will?"

"You could say that," she said.

"Why?" he asked.

"For one very selfish reason. I am an attorney. How would my clients view me if I married an older man—a very wealthy man—who died before his time and left everything to me? I had every tool available to make a fortune that way. Beauty—so they say—and a knowledge of every letter of the law, a doting husband. I pleaded with him to take me out of his will. I have never needed his money. I wanted a free and clear life after he passed on. I worked hard to convince him that he would *make me unhappy* by leaving his fortune to me. Everything he had known for his entire life told him that he should leave his fortune to the wife he loved."

"That would be a hard thing for a man," Emilio admitted. "Did you love him?"

"I don't know why I should answer. You're practically a stranger to me."

"True, and not true," he said.

She smiled very slightly. "I did feel affection for him. Not the grand passion he would have liked, but I was never dishonest with him about it. I will tell you the story of our courtship. I was twenty-five years old and starting my law practice when I met him. I was practicing in Phoenix and he found me by chance on a trip to the city. He was one of my early clients. I did an adequate job for him, but he immediately found more work for me. He found reasons to have meetings with me. I suspected that his interests were not completely concerned with business, but of course I wanted to ignore that and retain my professional image. He was making my practice very profitable, though, and it began to worry me. I was almost to the point where I felt I had to address the matter with him, but he brought it up first. He asked me to dinner and I accepted, thinking it would be the opportunity I needed to have a private discussion with him.

"Unfortunately," she continued, "he began the evening with a dozen long-stemmed roses, the most gallant and courtly manner imaginable, and a stream of such compliments that I could not mistake his intentions. I made the decision to tell him the truth, even if it meant losing his business. I had made the decision long ago to never marry. I had no interest in being a wife and bearing children. I could not pretend to be interested in that kind of life. It was nothing personal, as he was not an unattractive man, even though he was nearly twenty years my senior. So I told him all these things outright. Do you know what his reply was?"

"What was it?" asked Emilio.

"He said, 'Of course you do not love me yet. It is my job to make you love me. You will see. Just relax and enjoy it.' I explained to him again that I had no intentions of every marrying and that he could not hope for me to ever change my mind, but it didn't make a bit of difference. He did not see an insurmountable obstacle in anything I said."

"That's very Latin," said Emilio, "and very male."

"Well, that may be," said Francesca, "but it was disconcerting to me. We ended the evening by bargaining over how often he would be allowed to take me to dinner. I was tempted to become angry and to feel degraded by the experience, but he was a perfect gentleman, and I could see he was a good man. I finally agreed to once a month just to end the evening."

"And how long did that go on?" asked Emilio.

"Four years, punctuated by frequent business meetings when he could scarcely conceal his intentions. I began having office staff present at the meetings on any pretext—taking notes or running a projector—so that he would not feel so free to work on his courting while at the same time paying me a consulting fee for it. I felt awful! Can you imagine?"

"I can," confessed Emilio, but he was imagining more of what Senor Gordon felt than what Francesca felt.

"Gradually he wore me down, Emilio," continued Francesca. "I would never have guessed that about myself. I began to grow to like him, and to appreciate the way he treated me. I grew attached to it, even. He managed to make me confess this, and then he proposed. He told me he was certain I would eventually grow to love him, as we had come so far already, and he could think of no other woman. He begged me to have him for a husband, on the traditional bended knee. He offered me anything, everything. I explained to him that I was a career woman, I could not be a housewife, I could not be tied down with children, and none of it made a dent in his intentions. He told me I could continue my career as always, if only I would live with him and be his wife. He would tie no strings to me, expect nothing more of me than what I already was. He begged me to make him completely happy before he was too old to be happy. I gave in."

"And were you both happy?" Emilio asked.

"By all appearances," she said, "he was as happy as he claimed he would be. He kept his word to me completely. There never was a more consistent and predictable man. My affection for him grew, and I tolerated the situation well as long as he seemed to be happy. But I knew it was not the same for me as it was for him." She sighed and pulled a yellow rose from the vase at the table. "Now that he is gone, I am confused and re-assessing my life." She studied the rose silently for several minutes.

Emilio did not speak, waiting for her to begin again. "If I realized anything by becoming his wife and then his widow," said Francesca, "it was that he achieved something I have never achieved; something I have never even conceived of achieving."

"What is that?" asked Emilio.

"I'm not sure," she said. "I suppose that's why I'm looking at my life. Giraldo and I had so much in common, in some ways. The methodical, thorough approach I have taken to my profession seems similar to the way he approached the courtship with me. Except—"

"Yes?"

"Except that I am not nearly as happy being an attorney as he was being my husband. It makes me think I have missed something."

"Perhaps you have," said Emilio.

"Perhaps," she sighed. "It reminds me of a dream that I've never told anyone. I used to dream it only while sleeping, but now I even dream it while awake. It gives me a sensation that I like, and which gives me relief in moments of—I would say stress except that that's not quite the right word. Perhaps *heaviness* would be a better word. I fell heavy sometimes, tired of carrying around the framework that holds my knowledge; knowledge of my clients, their troubles, their sensitivities, the solutions to their problems, the solutions to their potential problems, and the pressures of the world on me to make me conform to some more acceptable idea of womanhood. Even Giraldo made me feel I was not an acceptable woman because he somehow treated me like–as wonderful as it was—like the woman that he imagined rather than like the woman that I really am.

"So if I felt this *heaviness*, then I would dream of feeling a *lightness* instead. I would dream of riding through the scrub on horseback—silly as it sounds— with the sun on my back and my notebook in a pouch. I felt free and light, and I was fascinated with all of life. Not just clients—humans—and paperwork and law, but the rest of life. Everything living. I stopped for every interesting cactus or bush, observed the ants and the scorpions with wonder, took notes, studied and was thrilled with the whole of it. Mostly, though, it was that sensation of being there, of riding through that land on horseback, feeling the sun and the wind and—" she suddenly looked up at him curiously.

"What?" he prompted.

"I found myself wanting to say the word 'love' but it didn't seem to fit. Is it possible to feel love for the desert? I'm not sure if it is love of the place of of the feeling of moving through the wind on horseback? Or of feeling free to do that? I don't know. It was such a feeling of lightness compared to the way I feel the rest of the time.

"Yet I am *comfortable* with the way I feel most of the time. I don't dislike it. It is a serious and responsible attitude toward life. I take my clients' needs seriously. I take my profession seriously. I try to do what is right. I know what I am doing, and I am going round and round in a little framework that I know inside out. Not like riding through the wind."

He let her think for several minutes.

"I wonder if life *should* be like that," she finally said. "Lightness, instead of heaviness, I mean. I had the impression, from everything I was taught and from everything I accepted as true, that this framework was the right thing to operate in. But perhaps the ecstasy that I saw in Giraldo's eyes when I agreed to marry him, perhaps that was his source of *lightness*. He was not supposed to court and marry a woman like me. He was supposed to marry a woman of his own class who would be a traditional wife to him. He ignored all that to marry me. I could never understand what gave him such delight, but if he felt what I have felt in my dreams—"

She stopped abruptly and stood out and went to the balcony. He followed her.

"What happened?" he asked.

"I don't know," she said. "Maybe I can tell you better tomorrow."

"All right," he replied. "I will meet you at noon. Is that all right?"

"Yes. Good bye, Emilio," she said, her back still towards him to hide her tears.

He was quite overcome himself. He felt he had tracked with her perfectly and had realized in the same instant as she had what it was all leading to. In that last silence he had heard from her expression the next ten minutes' worth of what she had not said. Francesca Gordon had never loved a man because the character of it fell outside of the framework of life as she conceived it. She had omitted it, even if unknowingly, from the construction of her current life. Her only clue to herself was the dream of riding through the desert on horseback. Was it something she had once done as a child? It didn't matter.

Emilio realized another thing. Giraldo Gordon had never been able to awaken love in his wife because he had loved her by his own definition and given her what he thought women wanted rather than what Francesca wanted. Giraldo had never even found out about her dream. *May I never make that mistake*, thought Emilio.

The next day at noon, Emilio arrived underneath Francesca's balcony on horseback, leading a second horse for Francesca. Each saddle was equipped with a pouch containing notebook, pencil, field guide, map, food and water. Emilio had dreamed of having her jump off the balcony into his arms in her excitement, but he was pleased with what really happened. She broke out into a smile of pure lightness, ran down to mount her horse, and they rode off into the desert.

The One I Sought

By Amit Kapoor

My eyes shone with hope
When I heard you say—
"I am with you."

With a heart beating louder,
And adrenalin pumping faster,
For a moment I felt,
My fate's own master.

No more pessimist ideas and
No more sleepless nights—I thought,
For, I had the love I wanted,
I had the one I sought.

You.

Uses for Tuba Cases

By Keenan Brookland, 2011

There comes a time for many people when the urge to express an attraction toward a person of the opposite sex—no matter how illogical it may be—gets the better of us.

When I decided I wanted to marry the next door neighbor boy at age 8, that wasn't so terribly illogical. He was capable, treated me with equality, and was a decent person. My mother was his babysitter so I knew his character thoroughly.

Then adolescence arrived.

One day I was walking down the hall at school and a very illogical feeling came over me when a particular person walked by. There really is going to be a tuba case in this essay; please be patient. At this point I did not know the name of the person or anything about him, but it soon dawned on me that it was the person my friend spoke disparagingly of because he teased her in 5th period. I found out his name and that he was on the varsity basketball team. He was six foot six—you couldn't miss him. I found out he was known as the biggest flirt in the school and hung out with the cheerleaders.

In other words, he was my opposite.

My friend asked me if I wanted to volunteer to sell snow cones at basketball games and that was something I would normally not be caught dead doing, but I agreed to do it.

I started giving my friend notes before she went to 5th period, knowing somehow that she would eventually let one fall into his hands by accident if I mentioned him frequently in the notes in a melodramatic manner.

It came to pass, through accidents of fate I no longer remember, that I sent him a note directly one day—something frivolous with a lot of teasing. He wrote one note back, which was to be the last note he ever wrote me. I didn't believe a word of it, because I knew that he was a "flirt;" however, I did memorize it. Then I tried to deliver some real communication via a second note—not just fluff and teasing but some actual thoughts about life. He never responded.

I was torn for a while between rejecting the whole thing as tragically impossible and trying to convince myself that there must be some logical reason why I felt the way I did. It was an obsession. I cured myself of it by transferring into the small 4th period math class he was in during the second half of the year. There were about eight people in the class and only two of us were girls. He flirted with the other girl in the class almost every class period, non-stop, except when she was absent.

As an aside, I looked him up many years later, under no obsession but just curious to see if I would have any better luck at getting him to communicate with me. I found an email address for him and he replied to my message. He had no recollection of who I was, but was polite. I told him I remembered him talking with the pretty red-haired girl through math class and he said he wished he hadn't done that. He said he tells his boys to pay attention in class.

Getting back to that high school year, it happened to be the year of the first ever girl's track team at my school. I was on the team, not because I had much ability in that area but because they were short on recruits and my two friends were on the team. One of them said she had a crush on a sophomore on the boy's track team. To divert attention from herself on this front, she began teasing me about him. I didn't realize that others overheard this and the false idea that the crush was mine and not hers spread to the whole girl's track team, and maybe the boy's track team as well.

One day the three of us decided that an anonymous love note should be written to him. It escapes me just how and why we decided that. I thought it was on my friend's behalf, but I volunteered to write the note because note-writing was my specialty. Our other friend volunteered to deliver the note discreetly by placing it in his tuba case. She was in band and so was he.

The next day there was a response from him. We were thrilled and read it eagerly. I remember only the line, "my love flows elsewhere," and I thought that was very poetic. I declared we had to write an answer to that. The next day my friend told me that when he discovered a second note in his tuba case, he approached her and said, "Did Keenan write this?"

I was horrified. This note was supposed to be from my friend, not me. I begged her to tell me that she had straightened him out on that point. Instead, she said she thought that I was the one who had the crush on him and that it was my motivation for writing the note. I, however, had been caught up in the aesthetic creation of the communication and not in any kind of crush.

The whole thing had backfired on me. After the required amount of agonizing over what I had done, it all blew over. My band member friend wrote an arrangement of *The Entertainer* for piano, trumpet, tuba, and piccolo, and we played it for the Honor Society banquet. Afterwards in the band room, the boy whose love flowed elsewhere offered to let me try his tuba. Playing the tuba is, after all, another form of communication so I gave it a shot. It may be the only time I will ever play a tuba—it was rather difficult!

Apparently he had forgiven me for the notes in the tuba case. He was a very sensible person. He had been in my English literature class the first half of the year and I'd read an essay he'd written. He was a good guy, and I'm sure he's doing well somewhere.

I learned not to try to speak for anyone else on the subject of romance, in or out of tuba cases.

Fortunately I never learned to stop communicating. When I finally began the courtship period for what became a very happy marriage, all my note-writing of earlier years went to a practical use. It so happened that we chose to do a great deal of our communication in writing, and learned about each other's interests, views, and desires for the future this way. He sent notes to me in envelopes decorated with speedily drawn sketches, and soon I was decorating my envelopes back to him. It has been a very creative liaison.

And that is how I came to be married to Slate Bender.

LOVE KNOWS NO BOUNDS

By Slate Bender

What's the Cause?

By Amit Kapoor

What's in you—that's not in me?
What's in me—that's not in you?
Then,
What's the cause,
That separates me from you?

What's the creed,
What the customs—
That have set us apart?

What's the deed,
What the nation
That have made us part?

What's the color of your blood,
That does not flow in my veins?
What monsoons you enjoy,
That do not wet me as rains?

What's the day, what the night,
That for me is dark—and for you bright?

Then,
What's the reason for our separation,
That cause only anguish and pain?

A Bird's View

By Amit Kapoor

A Bird.
O' yes, I'm but a bird.

I like to soar high,
And fly a little low,
I perch down on trees,
And swoop on the ground below.

I've seen the world at large,
Men, who over petty things get charged;
I've seen them praying,
And I've seen them slaying;

I've seen the flowers bloom, -
And the o'erspread gloom.
Was this the world He made?
And is this the life for which we prayed?

I'm but speechless,
My thoughts don't show—
I can't raise my voice,
And I can't raise a brow—

'coz I'm a bird, I know.

The Price of Freedom

By Keenan Brookland, 2000

If you spend part of a day sometime listening to the caliber of complaints around you in society, it might strike you that most are relatively minor.

We forget that we have had many freedoms handed to us on a silver platter by our ancestors and others who made it happen by giving us birth in the right place at the right time. I know someone who grew up in Viet Nam and did not have these freedoms.

When Bai was a young man he lost both legs below the knee. He was a member of the infantry in the Viet Nam war and had the misfortune of stepping on a land mine. He carried on and got married and had seven children.

His oldest child was about fourteen when he and his wife made a decision. Life was nearly intolerable. The government required him to report in each week and answer up at length about his activities for every minute of the past week. He and his fellows were under constant scrutiny and threat. No freedom. In America, however, he knew there was freedom to work at a job of one's choice, where more and harder work would mean more pay and a chance to make a life for oneself.

Bai and his wife decided to try to go to America in a boat. If the boat sank and the family drowned together, that was still better than living with no freedom.

He knew *nothing* about boating. He had been in the army, not the navy. He and a couple of other families got together and built a 30-foot boat with which they planned to sail the Pacific Ocean. In order to reach the ocean they had to navigate a river downstream for about an hour's journey. They divided up into three boats for this part of the journey, as overcrowded children and babies might start crying and alert police to their illegal escape. There were 52 of them in all; 27 of them were very young children or babies.

The boat was powered by a motor with about as much power as a lawnmower. It was a homemade boat. Chances of surviving the Pacific in this boat were too small to think about. They crept slowly down the river that night, keeping the motors as slow as possible to ensure they were not heard.

All went well until they were near the river's mouth. The police were alerted to the presence of the rear boat and captured several of the escapees. Three of those were Bai's children. They were his oldest children, aged 14, 12 and 7. He did not learn until later that they were threatened with gunfire, then tied together in the police stations with ropes around their hands and necks.

Once the rest of them were at the mouth of the river, having waited in the woods until all signs of danger were gone, they had to decide what to do. If they could get to America, they could always send back for the others later. They decided to go ahead.

The mother of his children wept so continuously that he worried they would yet be discovered. He reminded her many times that she needed to be quiet.

At last they were in the 30-foot boat, out on the ocean. In the course of their journey a large ship from Red China spotted them and sped over to them, then quickly by them in order to make the water as choppy as possible. They struggled with ten foot waves.

Only a few days out into the Pacific, the water grew alarmingly rough. Bai's handheld compass was not working at all as he had expected; it just spun around. He steered according to the sun, which was the only other navigational tool he had.

A large ship approached. He saw the American flag flying upon it and cried out for help. He and the others were taken aboard the *Black Gold,* an American-owned ship on its way to Malaysia. Soon after they boarded her, the homemade 30-foot boat was engulfed by waves and sank promptly.

In Malaysia they stayed at a refugee camp. There were tens of thousands of refugees crowded into one tiny island, sleeping twenty to a small room. The ocean was the only facility available for personal hygiene. Each week there were visits from consuls around the world, and opportunities for those who qualified to start new lives elsewhere.

Bai and his family were offered the opportunity to fly to Portland, Oregon. They were sponsored by a program in a Portland church that was designed to help refugees. They were given their first month's rent in a house, and lessons in English.

Bai and his wife found their first job at a local restaurant, doing the cleaning. The pay was $1.75 an hour, which was low even for 1985. They kept the job for two years, however, as it was better than living on welfare or having nothing. They not only had themselves and four of their children to support, but also the three children who had been left behind in Viet Nam. They found out by corresponding with Bai's mother that the three children had been imprisoned for months before being released. Bai sent money back to his relatives in Viet Nam every month for the care of his children. He also sent them a map, showing them how to escape.

One by one the three children arrived in Portland to join the rest of the family. Each and every one of Bai's children attended school and college. The youngest two are in college now. Bai beams with joy when he speaks of how he has turned his life from a nightmare of oppression into a life of having what all other Americans have: a house, a car, educated children; but most of all *freedom.* He says that money is not important next to that.

May you use your freedom well.

YOU WILL BE VERY HAPPY

By Slate Bender